Gloucest

Ghosts and Giggles

To Sheila.
love from Lyn xx

L. J. Cinderey

Lyn Cinderey

Copyright: Lyn Cinderey 2017

ISBN: 978-0-244-01382-0

Front cover Tony Le Mesmer Lee

Back cover Tony Marriot

ABOUT THE AUTHOR

This is my second book on my extensive experiences of the paranormal and am known locally as 'The Ghost Lady' still, even though I have now retired from my ghost walks and overnight paranormal investigations, although doing the odd one that interests me. Age, they say, is but a number but when you're awake and investigating dark, spooky places until the early hours of the morning, I can assure you, I DO feel my age. Stubbornness is what keeps me going.

Acknowledgements

Once again as in my first book: Paranormal Gloucester, I would like to thank all my friends that have been there for me.

Also To: Alan Myatt. Town Crier, Toastmaster & Master of Ceremonies & character actor. A true a loyal friend who has given me very, very, good advice regarding my books and ghost walks. Many many thanks to you Alan.

To Sue And Phil Tandy from The Robert Raikes House
Paul Soden from Cafe Rene and all the crew
My dear now departed friend A.M.
Nick from The Old Bell
Kirsty from The Old Bell
Samantha And Mark Cooke
Martin and Kay from The Dick Whittington

I would also like to thank all my friends everywhere
Special thanks go to

My husband Tony
Sons Shaun and Dean.
Moira and Paul Goddard
Pammie Harper
Terence Harper
Denise Badham
Nikki Yeates
Darren Thompson
David Mason
Tracey Stevens
Elaine Emerton
Leanne Yeates (Sadly now passed away)
Richard Butler

Bruce
Ed
Lisa Baskerville
David Baldwin
Shaun Moore
Angela Gillett
Norman Ferguson
And many many more. You ALL know who you are.

I was born and bred in Gloucester so I'm a local Gloucester Girl. As a child, I grew up like many children with loads of questions. But mine was a fascination, somewhat weird if you like, of the unknown, the mysteries of life. I used to draw Churches and crosses and grave stones all the time but never knew why.

Over the years, I have had several different experiences, some explained some unexplained. I believe we go through life to learn to be better people and to help each other through difficult times. Sadly, as we know, that is not always the case.

If we don't go through certain things, then how can we help and 'educate' for the want of a better word. It's like you telling someone how to do their job but not knowing anything about it. It's wasted and falls on deaf ears.

Since writing my first book Paranormal Gloucester, I have been encouraged to write another, so here it is. I do hope you enjoy it as much as you did my first one. So sorry for the long, long wait. So many things have changed and happened to me in the past few months, both spiritually and mentally. I am told by people that are far more qualified than myself that the Universe is changing, for the better I hope. All the pain and anguish and upheaval people are going through right now is all to do with Karma and our future. Sounds quite frightening, doesn't it? Something out of Steven Spielberg's books springs to mind.

I do believe most strongly that things are meant to be and that there is a plan for us all and it is already mapped out for us. It is then down to us to choose which path to take, hopefully the right one. But we do have that choice. My choice is to live life to the full, to do what I love best, to explore and investigate places that have a story to tell. To meet new people and experience their stories that they have to tell and then record them.

In my last book, I told many tales from in and around Gloucester and stories people very kindly sent me. I will continue to do this but on a more wider scale, from outside Gloucester and beyond. Also, people's own encounters of the paranormal as well as my own and our team of paranormal investigators. We called ourselves G.A.P.S. (Gloucester Active Paranormal Society), a team of like-minded people looking for evidence into the paranormal and ghostly goings on around us. Sadly, we are no longer formed as a team but sometime some of our team members and other friends that frequently joined us on investigations still meet up and go on investigations together.

Nikki Yeates, Leanne Yeates (sadly now passed away but never forgotten), Elaine Emerton, Richard Butler, Darren Thompson, Dave Mason, Tracey Stevens, Bruce Ed Straughn, Paul Goddard, Martin Gillott, Johnathan Chater, Nicky Lynch, Nessa Haych, Nellie Lisa Woods, Mitchey Jayne Corinne Dyer, Zoe Tandy, Mitch Maher, Helen Adair, Carol Beasmore, Carol Vickers, Janet O'carroll, Hayley Yendall, Oh yeh, and me.

Yeh right! Some of you might say. Well that is entirely up to you. As I have said many times, we have all got the right to free will. I will NOT preach to you my own beliefs, just letting those that want to know by writing this book. Our team have investigated many places, some of which was already recorded in my first book, some of it after my book was published and is still going on today. So some venues will be mentioned again, but will be all new stories.

These are some of the places we have investigated. We have also investigated private homes. Cafe Rene, The New Inn, The Old Bell, The Crosskeys, Robert Raikes House, The Westgate, The Pig In The City, The Dick Whittington, Woodchester Mansion, Cotters bar shoe Shop and British Heart Foundation. The Ram Inn, Littledean Jail, Littledean House Hotel, The Station Hotel, A.G. Meeks Shoe Shop, Bookends Bookshop, Age Concern Shop, The Folk Museum, The Waterways Museum, The Services Club, Tutbury Castle, Derby Jail, Ruthin Jail, Hunters Hall, Caesars Night Club and Condover Hall.

I have also added what has been posted in our local paper. These are but a few of many articles and events I did and the Citizen reported it. The Citizen, I thank them for their continued support. Spooky happenings in Gloucester pub captured on CCTV Wednesday, June 2nd 2010. FALLING pint glasses, moving cutlery and footsteps on the stairs sparked a ghostly investigation at a Gloucester pub. Spooky happenings have been reported at the New Inn in Gloucester – and experts claim the past month has been one of the busiest times at the haunted hot spot. In the past, people have claimed to have seen spectres of children playing in the courtyard, a nanny watching them and also a blacksmith in the grounds of the 600-year-old pub. But the most recent – and most spectacular – event was captured on CCTV cameras this week when a pint glass fell from a table in the bar, with nobody within touching distance of it.

Mark Cooke has been landlord at the pub, in Northgate Street, since February 2010. He said: "I was a bit dubious of the paranormal before seeing that footage, but there's no denying what happened. "There is definitely something going on here, there's no doubt about it." He admitted other strange things had been happening recently – enough to warrant a full scale overnight investigation on Friday. "We had 10 cameras set up all around the place on Friday and we captured a few things," he added, "For example, we saw some cutlery moving in the restaurant. It is quite scary. A couple of weeks ago I got a call from a member of staff at 2am asking me if I was still in the pub because he could hear footsteps on the stairs – but I was in bed at the time. I wouldn't say I was a 'believer' but I can tell you this, when you're locking up at 3am in the pitch black, it's enough to make the hairs on the back of your neck stand up."

Lyn Cinderey, of Gloucester Active Paranormal Society (Gaps), believes that the current activity in Gloucester is the busiest it's ever been. She said: "There is a lot going on at the moment. We held a seance in the New Inn on Friday night and we had a Brian Turner come through to speak to us, and he may have been the one who pushed the pint glass over. He said he was a blacksmith and he was born in 1434 and he died in 1465". There have also been reports of whispering, quiet music being played and knocking. The video showing the falling pint glass can be seen on The Citizen website thisisgloucestershire.co.uk

Step inside spirit world. SPOOKY stuff is afoot at Woodchester Mansion when the Gloucester Active Paranormal Society hosts an investigation of things that go bump in the night. Brave souls can go along at 8pm on Friday until 4am the following morning to search for the spirits which reputedly haunt the unfinished Victorian Gothic mansion.

I also love doing events for various Charities as G.G.W. Gloucester Ghost Walks. Parents and their newborn babies got a scary but generous visit from the members of the Gloucester Ghost Walks. Lyn Cinderey and her scarer's (who both wish to remain anonymous) dropped into Gloucestershire Royal Hospital's Special Care Baby Unit on New Year's Eve to donate a year's worth of collections. Lyn said: "I take a small donation from everyone who go on the walks and put it in a sealed tin all throughout the year. Then on New Year's Eve I open the tin and donate it to the charity we have chosen for the year. Last year we decided on Scoo-b-doo and we went along to give them the cash. We raised £122.54 and got to see some of the babies and mums there. They were all so small. I thought my scarer's might be a bit too much for them but I was assured the little ones wouldn't mind." Lyn presented the money to matron of Neonatal Services, Wendy Owen.

Ghost walk 'survivors' take home certificates. CERTIFICATES of survival are on offer for all those who go the distance on a Gloucester ghost walk. Ghost walks were run on a regular basis in the city, delving into Gloucester's spookiest hot spots Everyone received a certificate of survival after the walk and for an extra £1 per person the certificate can be framed.

Shire Hall staff spooky lunch break. Staff from Shire Hall in Gloucester enjoyed a spooky twist to their lunch break this week. The city's first lady of the paranormal world; Lyn Cinderey, led 50 workers around the city on one of her famous ghost walks on Tuesday. "They absolutely loved it," said LYN, who is adorned with a black cape and hat for the walks. "I took them around the main spooky hot spots in the city centre and showed them the room in the New Inn pub where the pint of beer mysteriously fell off the table. In May, CCTV footage in the pub captured a pint glass falling from a table with no-one near it. I think they learned quite a lot to be honest, and a lot of them said they would like to do it again" added Lyn. "I hopefully educated them a bit about their city too. I taught them that it's worth looking around and up at the buildings from time to time as well."

A thrilling kids' party. Children get chills and thrills at the Halloween celebrations this year. A spooky party for youngsters is being hosted by Gloucester Ghost Walks at The New Inn, in Northgate Street, on Friday October 29. The event will start at 6pm and finish at 8pm. The cost of a ticket is £3 per child and accompanying parents. It is, of course, fancy dress and there will also be prizes, games, zombie dancing, music, raffle, apple bobbing, a marshmallow eating competition and refreshments. Put a spooky spin on Christmas

PEOPLE in Gloucester can put a spooky spin on their Christmas dinner this year. Gloucester Ghost Walks is offering its services during the festive period for those with an interest in the paranormal. All people have to do is decide a date and a location for their Christmas meal and contact Gloucester Ghost Walks, and they will do the rest.

Ghostly goings-on on walk for youngsters in holidays KIDS can look forward to a spooky summer holiday. Children generally love to hear scary stories about spooks and spectres, and now they will get a chance to find out more about their local friendly ghosts.

Gloucester Ghost Walks, run by Lyn Cinderey, is offering a children's ghost walk over the school holidays. For £2 per child and £3 per adult, people can spend an hour walking around some of Gloucester's most haunted and historic locations. The walks start from July 27 at 1pm until 2pm from The New Inn Courtyard until August 31. Children wanting to go on the walk can pay on arrival or contact Lyn Cinderey in advance on 07908 552855.

Launch of pub book, the story of Gloucester's historic pubs will come to life in a new book about the spooky side of the city.

The Story of Gloucester's Pubs, written by Darrel Kirby, will be officially launched on July 13 at the New Inn, one of the most historic pubs in the center. It identifies more than 600 pubs, going back as far as the 13th century. Some are linked to Edward II and Henry III, historical celebrities such as Dick Whittington and famous ships like Sir Francis Drake's Golden Hind and the Pilgrim Fathers Mr Kirby will be joined on the night by the ghost hunter Lyn Cinderey. Copies of the book will be on sale at discounted prices from

7:30pm.

Big snooze in BRAVE fundraisers can take part in a sponsored sleepover in the Eastgate Viewing Chamber in Gloucester. The event is being held to raise money for the City Museum and The Pied Piper Appeal. All you need is £25 sponsorship. To enter call Lyn Cinderey on 07908 552855. Rare visit to chamber.

HISTORY

Fans can take a trip down into some of Gloucester's most ancient foundations. Lyn Cinderey, from Gloucester Ghost Walks, will be inviting people to join her in a rare opportunity to go inside the Eastgate viewing chamber outside Boots. The chamber currently offers visitors a glance at the historic Roman East Gate tower, which dates back more than 1,500 years. There are plans in place to replace the chamber, thought by many to be old and unsightly, with glass panelling which visitors can walk over. It is hoped the renovation of the chamber will offer a better view of the historic monument. The tour inside the chamber will go ahead on Friday night from 7pm to 8pm. Entry costs £5 for adults and £1 for children over seven.

Lyn Cinderey, who leads weekly walks through the city centre, said: "Gloucester is certainly a spooky place, there's a lot of history here. There are so many ghost stories and sightings, it's almost unbelievable.

"Cafe Rene in Southgate Street is one of the most haunted places. Several people have seen shadows in the basement which used to be connected by a tunnel to St Mary de Crypt Church. "When we did a night-time investigation, we heard monks chanting and there were also lots of bright blue orbs around the area (orbs are the first manifestation of a ghost). "When the landlord was packing up the till takings one night, after everyone had left, he felt a hand on him and dropped the takings in fright. But when he went back the next day the money was still there. If it had been a human, the money would have been taken, but ghosts don't need money."

There are also believed to be ghosts at the New Inn in Northgate Street where horrible whispering has been heard.

At AG Meek shoe shop, in Westgate Street, staff have smelled the perfume thought to be that of a ghost and heard a spoon being stirred in a teacup when no one could be seen.

At nearby Bookends bookshop, a monk is rumoured to have murdered a woman and a slim, young man with short dark hair, who is always carrying a book, has been seen many times at a shed at the back of the shop.

City council leader Councillor Paul James, said: "It doesn't surprise me that we've come in the top 10, given the number of historic buildings we've got. "Being highlighted in the top 10 can only improve tourism in the future." The

Supernatural Britain report was commissioned by Warner Home Video to mark the release of TV series Supernatural Season Three on DVD. What I am trying to do is record our history for future generations, telling them as well as showing them what it was like in 2010 -2011. Our young people today are the future for tomorrow. They will be leaders, Scientists Historians etc and Hopefully Care about this City as I have. The things we have found about the City of Gloucester will be preserved forever in books, and on Dvd's. We have long been envied of our Heritage, so let's be proud and Loud about It and show everyone what we are about.

Many, many people have said to me, on my walks, talks, and paranormal nights that they love to explore the unknown, the mysteries uncovered, the excitement of going on ghost walks and overnight paranormal investigations. Our group was called G.A.P.S. (no longer formed). I am proud to say had a different approach to most paranormal groups. Although wanting to learn and experience ghost and all things that go bump in the night, we truly respect the dead. We do not expect them to 'perform' on request, after all, it is not a circus or show. They are not there for our amusement, they are there because they want to be.

We send a lot of love out on our paranormal nights. We pray and ask that spirits may come through if they wish, just to show us that there is life after death. Many times, when we have gone on a 'haunted' location, we don't just attract the spirits of the place, but also, we have found that our own loved ones come through, even for the people that attend our events. This is truly amazing, magical, and an honour to experience this. We all know it our heart of hearts that our aim is to Investigate.........Not HUNT...BUST or anything else that usually labels paranormal groups. We all love what we do, and never provoke ghosts to appear if nothing is happening. If they want to appear they would. Put yourself in their shoes. If you haunt an area, building etc for whatever reason, wouldn't you get fed up of people coming along asking the same old questions and expecting you to appear all the time? I know I would. I would probably say something like 'oh here we go again. Why don't you lot bog off and leave us in peace'. But if you have respect and treat people like you would have when they were alive, just think of the difference this may make. If not, then so be it.

Introduction

The paranormal, the spiritual, the unknown, the supernatural, call it what you will. Most human beings are intrigued by this. Is it because it's different, unusual, or something else that seems to attract us to these subjects?
I personally have been asked several times, when did I get into all this?

Well, I think it started at a very early age, not exactly sure how old I was but about when I was six or seven.
I always remember in our living room we had an upright black piano. I loved to tinkle on it, I used the word tinkle because I couldn't play, but I liked to think I could, much to the annoyance of the family.

I remember I always liked to tinkle sombre tunes, church like music, and I would always cry, tears running down my face, so that I could no longer see the keys.

What a strange person, I hear you saying. Yes, well to a degree I agree with you, but was this a starting point as to what lay ahead for me? Of course, at that age I had no idea. I often drew Churches, and Gravestones as well. Now she has lost the plot you're all saying.
Ok maybe I had, maybe it was an omen, I don't know.

All I know is when I was 11 years old, my Dad was killed by a hit and run driver on his way to work. Dad was riding his bicycle in the early hours of the morning, when a car hit a moped driver who then knocked Dad off his bike and was taken to hospital where he died later.

Yes, very tragic and sad, and you cannot imagine what was going through my 11 year old mind.

My sister Maureen, but she preferred to be called Mo (sadly Mo has now passed away) and I were told later on in the morning while we were having assembly at school.

The most disturbing and horrific thoughts came into my head, as the night before Dad's death, he had given me such a hiding because he found out that I was picking up dog ends off the ground and smoking them. Dad was very caring, and loving, but also very strict at times. After I had the lecture and the hiding, I was sent to bed, where I wished my dad was dead. He heard me and came back up to my room, and I received another hiding.

Now, people that are reading this, don't get all uppity at this, because in those days, a good hiding never hurt us, and it was only ever used in extreme conditions, so don't be condemning my dad.

I loved my dad, more than he may have ever known. I was a daddy's girl, always followed him everywhere. i certainly did deserve that hiding, in fact thanks to my dad I do not smoke today.

What I am trying to say is, the next day when my dad was killed. How do you think I felt, an 11 year old child wishing her dad was dead, then he was? Omg! What kind of power did I have, how could I do this?

Thirty years I held that in, thirty years! Was it my fault? Was it fate? Was this why I drew grave stones and Churches, and cried when I 'tinkled' on the piano? Who knows, I will let you decide this.

I know what I have been through, two years of counselling, and yet it's still remains with me. But I also now believe everything that I have gone through in my life has made an impact, a purpose or made me a stronger person.

Some people can go through life with absolutely nothing wrong with them health wise or mentally and I envy them. But are they happy? In my experience, most of them, no they are not. Why?

I believe those of us that have gone through mental and physical illnesses have had to go through it so we can help others. Because we can cope, because we are stronger, because we have proved this by surviving the trials and tribulations of life.
We are thankful for what we have.
Is this destiny, fate or just my rantings? This is what I personally believe in and all that I do in my life now, is to love and help my fellow mankind, in a way that only I know how to do. If I can make someone smile or believe in themselves or to look around at what we have then I am extremely happy and content.

This is why I love running my ghost walks, the paranormal overnight investigations and now our Merlin Clairvoyant nights and psychic suppers. All connected like a jigsaw that has been forming many years ago, and I am now putting the final pieces in.

This book, not only explores the 'paranormal encounters ' of Gloucester, but also of other people's experiences around Gloucester and even far beyond, people that I have met and shared their stories with me, as I have just shared my story with you.

This time I have added all the funny things that have happened to me and to my friends and people that have been on my walks and tours, just to prove in a way, life is not all doom and gloom.

I would also like to mention that at the time of writing this book some of the people I have mentioned have moved away from Gloucester but their stories and their help have still been appreciated by me.

 A very special mention and dedication too, for my dear sister Mo Perry, who passed away December 17th, 2012 and my dear friend Leanne Yeates. Also, my dear friend A.M.
All gone to the Big House where we will see them when it is our turn.
I do hope you like my second book. God bless and love to you all.

Lyn xx

My Own Opinion.

I have spoken to many people over the years about 'Ghosts' listened to their stories and ideas and I have, in my own opinion, recently became more and more aware of 'Spirit' helping us on our journey of life. A lot of you are now thinking, she has just said ghosts, now spirits, so what is the difference?

Well again, in my own opinion, and I say this because I know there are lots of Sceptics out there (I am married to one lol) who don't believe in either. Lovingly called Grumpy as all my friends know.

To me a ghost is someone that lived then died and their energies live on, a bit like when you see an aeroplane in the sky then it leaves a vapor trail behind. The plane has gone, out of sight, but the vapor trails remains for a while. That is how I explain ghosts.

For whatever reason ghosts stay here on the Earth plane is down to that person that once had human form and what life they led.

A Spirit to me is US I believe. I believe we are all spirit first inside a human body so that we can be seen and heard etc. When the body or shell dies, our spirit lives on.

I also believe in a sense we are recycled. Don't laugh. Well ok go on then, I did at first. Why not? Everything else is recycled, why not us?
We have the option to come back to Earth for whatever reason you deem or stay on other plains to progress or to heal or to help others to cross over.

I have said many, many times to people that when it is my turn I would love to come back to earth but as a ghost. Not to haunt anyone, but to take a look around all over the World at different places that I cannot do in human form.
Especially going into stately homes and mansions, having a good nosy round. Now now, not like that...lol. Just seeing different things of interest. And also go back in time to see our history and did we get it right or wrong?

To look at medieval Gloucester and see how it really was. Am I being over ambitious? Who knows, the possibilities could be endless, and what fun.

Bringing you all back down to Earth now, I wonder how many more people feel like I do? Haha, ok not many.

We all have our beliefs, our ways, our standards etc. but at the end of the day we will all be called back to maybe start again. Undo what has been wrong, be better people, stronger, happier people in our beliefs and strive for a better world without wars, starvation, abuse to children or animals.

All these recessions going on. Why is it? Have we got greedy? have we become selfish? I believe we have.

That is why a lot of people today are looking for ways to feel better about themselves, better towards others. But which way do we turn? Our instincts tell us back to basics.

Back to Spirit, back to our psychic abilities, which are all natural. We are all psychic, we have just got lost on our journeys through life. If we can feel that again, the LOVE would flow through us, we would again be connected to what I believe we started out to be. Human BEINGS.

Once we start believing in ourselves then we can believe in others then we can hear our helpers and spirit guides and become psychic again, the power to help each other.

Sorry if to some of you if that seemed like preaching, it was not intended to, it is just the way I feel and wanted to share it with you all.

The collection of stories and people's own experiences they have encountered are to follow. Surely they can't all be wrong or deluded. Something or someone is guiding us. We have a path to follow in our time on earth but it is up to us to follow which path we take.

I do hope you enjoy mine and their stories.

My choice is to live life to the full, to do what I love best, to explore and investigate places that have a story to tell. To meet new people and experience their stories that they have to tell. And then record them.

My very first full blown apparition and how my paranormal journey began.

Caesar Nightclub London

Ruth Ellis, the last woman to be hung in Britain. She worked at Caesar's in 1948 when it was called The Locarno.
And now she haunts the club. The Club has now been demolished.

Ruth Ellis was part of the Soho nightclub scene of 1950's London. She was a hostess at a nightclub.

In 2000, I went to Caesar Night Club and met with other friends that were interested in Most haunted and the paranormal. We went to see a questions and answers show with The most Haunted Team and Derek Acorah.
After the show, the Most Haunted team went and we were all left to do our own investigating around the club.

I chose to go up on the balcony above the ballroom with my friend Nicky Lynch. All the lights were turned off except the small emergency lights above the fire doors, so everywhere else was pitch black.

I had my camcorder running but couldn't see a thing. It wasn't a very good one, and not being very technical minded I hoped it would do and at least record any sounds.

Nicky was walking just ahead of me, and I called out to her "Where was the area Ruth Ellis has been seen?" She said, "Just up around the kitchen area."

I carried on filming, when all of a sudden, I came across a doorway that was well lit up and this woman was standing there. I said a few choice words like 'oh dear, you frightened me'. Yeh right, course I did. Anyway, you can guess what I really said. Plus, I dropped my camcorder as I was so shocked at seeing her and so clearly, but luckily, I did have the strap around my neck, so it was still filming, albeit the floor, but did record our voices.

She put her finger up to her lips and said "sshhhh, there's people down there, doing a seance." I was still shocked and said, "What did you say?" She repeated what she had just said. I said "Oh! Sorry" and walked off.

I never mentioned to Nicky or anyone else what had happened. We carried on walking round and joined other groups doing vigils until the early hours.

At 6am I had to catch the train back to Gloucester. We all said our goodbyes and off I went.

When I got home, I was exhausted and went straight to bed, where I slept for 15 hours, yes, 15 hours.
When I finally woke up, I immediately remembered about the

woman I saw, and I was sweating and started thinking all about what had happened, trying to make sense of it all.

Who was she? Why was it all lit up around her yet everywhere else was pitch black? Why didn't my friend see her? Was it a trick played on me by other people? Why didn't I tell Nicky or anyone else for that matter? All these things were going round and round in my head.

I rang around everyone I could and asked them if they had played this trick on me. Everyone said no way would they have done that.

I asked Nicky did she see her or hear her? She said No.

I said to Nicky "Why on earth didn't I say something to you?" Normally anything anyone sees or hears are quick to tell the others, but I never.

The only thing she did say, which made it even creepier to me, was that she said she noticed how quiet I had gone, and that is not like me. Yeh, yeh, all those that know me are now nodding their heads, right?

Anyway, for months this eluded me. My camcorder had recorded our voices on there and I sent my tape away to be analysed by experts. The result came back that it was indeed my voice and a spirit voice. Wow!
I described who I saw to several people and they said it was Ruth Ellis, and the area I saw her was where she used to work.

The only rational explanation for me keeping quiet was that I went into what I call, a mini shock. My eyes saw her, my ears heard her yet my mind was not accepting her existence until I had time to rest and take it all in.

I will NEVER forget that experience.

Again, there will be people that have their own explanations of what happened. Well that is fine, that is their right. As for me, I was there, they were not.

Colin Byrne story at Cafe Rene

Colin has worked at Cafe Rene on and off for many years. He has told me some of the things that have happened there.

He was arranging some chairs in the restaurant with another person one day and they lined the chairs up by the tables. When they both returned on their last trip, all the previous chairs that they had neatly place under the tables were all leaning against the tables. Each of them blamed each other or someone else playing a prank on them, but found out no one had. They were freaked out by this and could not explain it.

David Gardener's story of 34 Lipson Road, Cheltenham

Strange noises have been heard in David's house many times which he cannot explain. His son is only 7 years old and has seen things that no one else can.
David's 2 year old daughter was sat at the top of the stairs one night holding her favourite toy and staring down the stairs. Her parents looked up at her because when she wakes up in

the night she usually comes down the stairs. But that night she didn't and she was biting her favourite toy elephant and not moving.
David and his wife then saw another little girl on the stairs sat right next to their daughter, then suddenly disappeared.

David said he has always been a non-believer, but after all the recent unexplained events he feels that someone or something is in his house. However, he said he did not feel threatened by it just unsure of what was happening and why.

David and his family have lived there for 2 years but in the past year a lot of unexplained things have been happening.

He told me that the house was about 60 years old.

David's daughter Page wakes up every night at 11.30pm then after 2 hours she goes back to bed. She has become very clingy and always wants a cuddle before she settles back into bed.

What or who wakes Page up?

I did an investigation there with some colleagues and we had a very high EMF reading, but put it down to a lot of electricity in the area. But still had a very heavy feeling, in fact a few of us had headaches all the time we were there, but went as we left the house.

We sat and did meditation on the children's beds (the children were not in the house this night), and I got the impression of a family that used to live there. A man, a lady and a little girl. David said this was correct. I had the feeling too that the little girl was very poorly and died young. David confirmed this also, even though I had never been there before and knew nothing of the previous occupants. A couple of the neighbours had also been experiencing odd things happening, but no one really knew what it was, just a heaviness and as if someone was watching them.

We have not heard from David or his family since. I do hope things have settled down for them.

Over 21 years now I have been arranging paranormal overnight investigations and 14 years running ghost walks. it has not always been doom and gloom, in fact, here are some of the funnier times that I have encountered.

Tutbury Castle

I was in the toilet that is inside the great hall at the castle when I heard this horrible moaning sound coming from behind the wall. I was well spooked out at the time until I realized it was then men's toilet and some poor man was having a somewhat stressful time on the loo. As I came out from the ladies, he also came out from the gents. I am not sure who had the redder face, me or him.

Another time at Tutters, as I called it back then, my colleagues and I were trying to get a little sleep on the floor of the great hall after having an eventful night of ghost hunting, thinking of all the 'spooky' places and noises we heard. I suddenly heard in the distance what sounded to me like a baby crying. Another colleague of mine also heard it. It kept up for quite some time and sounded like it came from the downstairs area. I could not contain myself any longer and had to go and look. As I went down the stairs and then went outside, the noises had stopped. Bloody typical, I said to myself. I noticed it was getting light outside and the views from the castle across the valley were stunning. Deep in thought and pretending (as you do) for a brief moment that this was my home a cry came out directly behind me. Jesus, did I bloody jump, only to realize it was a sodding peacock that had been locked up in a cage for the night to protect it from the foxes. I shouted at it and said, "gas mark bloody 5 for you today my friend!"

Woodchester Mansion

A fantastic place and very spooky. I was with a team of ghost investigators one night and we were all heading towards the very 'haunted ' kitchen area. A male member of the team Johno, was just walking in front of me into the kitchen when he came running back towards me, screaming like a banshee that he had seen the ghost of the cook that haunts there staring straight at him. I pushed the poor bloke back into the room and said, "get back in there then, that's what we bloody well came for". The poor man became a gibbering wreck the rest of the evening.

On our Gloucester ghost walks we have had some really funny experiences happen. One night, my 2 scarers were waiting for me and my party of people to come past them at the infirmary arches at the cathedral. Both of them were each hidden behind a pillar when suddenly they both jumped out screaming at this poor unsuspecting person, thinking it was me. It was not, it was the dean of Gloucester. Suffice to say he was not a happy chappy and we are now banned from that area.
St. Michaels tower, before civic trust took it over, was a place

one of my scarers used to hide in. He went ahead of me and my party to open the tower and hide behind a door, to jump out on people. I came around the corner by Starbucks, with approximately 40 people, which was the main entrance then, only to find my scarer coming out from behind some dustbins in the alley way there. I shouted at him and said "What are you doing there? You're supposed to be inside." He answered back in a very gruff voice "You gave me the wrong bloody key, I couldn't get in". Everyone roared with laughter and thought it was part of the act, but it wasn't.

Another time my scarer was leaving the tower all dressed in his usual scary outfit after frightening people, when a police car went past. It went down Eastgate Street, clocked him and reversed back, asked him what he was doing and he said "I'm the Gloucester ghost". The policeman said "Oh, ok" and drove off, not looking back.

Another time, again in the tower, my scarer was waiting behind the door that leads up the stone steps to the tower when he jumped out on my party. A man that was standing right by the door fled out in terror, pushing his wife out the way, nearly knocking her to the ground to get outside. She was not amused.

There is an alley off Westgate Street called pinch belly alley. My scarer, Pammie Harper, my lovely friend, was waiting to scare people when, just before I arrived, two policemen came rushing towards her. She quickly took her mask off and said, rather bemused and scared herself, "I'm only doing a ghost walk. I'm the scarer." The policemen apologized to her, and said they thought she was one of the thieves that had just stolen some lead off a roof just by the alleyway door. Like a true trooper though, Pammie continued to scare people after, rather more loudly than usual this time.

The Dick Whittington Public House was our venue one night for a clairvoyant night. We were all sat around listening to 2 mediums that were talking about spiritual matters, when all of a sudden the one lady stopped, and looked across at me and said that there was a man (ghost) lurking around us and was listening and waiting to do something menacing and we all were to be aware of him and watch out. Some of the audience asked if they could take pictures. The medium said, "Yes of course", so the flashing started. Now, now, not that kind of flashing.

I was watching and then felt rather odd (odder than usual) and was getting really frustrated and angry. But why? And at what? All of a sudden, I heard myself shout in a rather loud man's voice "Stop flashing!" I immediately realized that it had come from my mouth, but at the same time couldn't believe it. Everyone in the room nearly shit themselves, then I said, "Was that me? Oh my god!"
They all shouted back "Yes it was you but in a man's voice."
I was in shock and kept saying no way, no way, and we then all started to laugh as the medium said, "I did warn you he was up to something."
"Yeh, too bloody right" I said, "but I didn't expect him to use my voice."

One of the most funniest moments, which a lot of people who were there on the night will never let me forget, will you Mitchy Jayne, was when we were doing an overnight investigation at the new Inn.

There were approximately 20 people that night, some of them were already in other rooms doing vigils. I took a small group up into an old attic part and told them all to be very careful as it is very old and hardly used. Everyone did as I asked and walked steadily on the beams in the attic. I was last up and immediately slipped off a beam and my one leg went straight through the floor. So, if you can imagine this, my left leg is in a room underneath, my body is still in the bleeding attic. I fell to the floor holding my torch, looking down into what I thought was a secret room that I had just partially entered. I was so excited and was telling the 2 ladies that I thought I'd found another room and it was horribly dark and dirty down there and the wallpaper was rather dark and drab. When they both said, "let's have a look then", to which they did, they got up laughing their socks off again, telling me that it was not a secret room but a bedroom and it was dark and shabby looking because of the 600-year-old wattle and daub that I had just disturbed.

"Oh shit", I said "what have I done...get me up.... get me up" I was shouting. By this time everyone else had heard all this commotion and came to see what all the noise was about. I was finally pulled out, looking like I had just swept a bloody chimney and hobbled down the stairs, got the key to the room from the manageress who was laughing as much as everyone else, and we all went into the room, to find a massive hole in the ceiling in the corner of the bedroom. We turned the lights on and the whole room was black, the bed, the carpet, the TV. I really thought I was going to get banned from there but luckily, I wasn't. That put a whole new meaning to me putting my foot into it.

Ben Portman's story; Gatcombe: Cottage near Forest of Dean.

Ben's mum had an old record player where you had to physically put the arm across for it to play. She was cleaning and the record player started up on it's on. The record playing was called the highway man, which seemed rather odd at the time. This was in the cellar. She also saw shadows out of the corner of her eye. His dad used to say it was all a load of rubbish.

When Ben was about three years old he kept waking up, and screaming that there was a man at the bottom of his bed. He described what he looked like and his brother Andrew, who was 18, used to wake up in the same room and Ben would climb into bed with Andrew. Andrew also said he saw at the top of the door where there was a window, a guy looking down at them with a big brimmed hat on.

Years later, after moving away, Ben went back there with all his family to church and other places and he saw people that still lived there when they were there. They told them that there was a woman who used to live there and her husband worked away a lot. Going back 100 years ago, there were some steps in the garden and the lady dropped her baby and the baby died and she threw the baby down the well. Her husband found out and didn't take to this very well at all and swore that he would protect and look after the next child born into that house. Tracing back, Ben said there had not been another child born into the house until he was born there.

So, was this the man that Ben and his brother saw?
Ben moved to Tewkesbury and has never seen that man again or his brother.

Gloucester Prison

One of my lifelong ambitions was fulfilled today, Sunday February 17th, 2013, when I was allowed inside Gloucester Prison. I Hasten to add, not as an inmate though, lol. The prison was due to be closed at the end of March 2013. A massive thank you to my dear friend Darren Thompson (Ex Prison Officer) for choosing me out of only three people that he was allowed to take in to the prison today at 1pm this afternoon for the grand tour.

A little history of the prison

A category B adult local prison and young offender remand centre, originally built in 1782 and substantially rebuilt in 1840. The original single large wing still holds those remanded or recently convicted. A wing for young offenders was added in 1971 and gate, administration, visits and stores block built in 1987.

Executions at Gloucester.

Prior to 1792, executions had taken place at the nearby village of Over and the condemned were conveyed to the gallows in carts, sitting on their own coffins. After this date, hangings were carried out using a "New Drop" style gallows erected on the roof of the prison gatehouse and continued on the new gatehouse roof when it was built in 1826. Between 1792 and 1864, 102 prisoners were hanged in public, comprising 94 men and eight women. There were no executions at all between 1839, when William Davis was hanged on the 20th of April for the murder of John Butt and July 1864. The next and last public execution at Gloucester was carried out on the 27th of August 1864 when 55-year-old

Lewis Gough was to die for the murder of Mary Curtis.

A further 17 people (16 men and one woman) were hanged within the prison between 1872 and 1939.

The first private hanging took place on the 8th of January 1872 when 20-year-old Frederick Jones was put to death by William Calcraft for the murder of his girlfriend, Emily Gardner, on a raised scaffold in the prison yard. This was the same gallows as had previously been used on the roof. There were steps the prisoner had to climb to reach the four-foot-high platform. For the triple hanging of Edward Butt, Mary Ann Barry and Edwin Bailey in 1874, Robert Anderson, the hangman, asked for a pit to be dug to allow the gallows platform to be level with the yard. It is thought that this arrangement persisted until 1912.

Ever since I was a young child I have always been fascinated by Gloucester Prison. My mother used to take me to the dentist which was somewhere in Barrack Square. We had to walk up some steel steps to go to the dentist and on coming out I always went up and touched the big prison doors. I know, I'm sad and always wanted to go inside the prison (not as a prisoner). Well, today that wish came true. Nearly 60 years I have had to wait but it was well worth it. All thanks to my dear friend Darren Thompson, who, until the end of March 2013 was a prison officer there. Darren was allowed to take in three friends or family for an hour's tour, the last day any of the public will ever go in there. So, for me this was a truly remarkable piece of history not to be missed, plus of course my ambition to visit it.

Darren invited his fiancé Nicola Yeates and Yvonne, her Mother. I have to say it was a very sad time for Darren and his fellow colleagues, some of which have been there for years. I felt their sadness and somewhat anger at the closure of the prison. I cannot blame them by the way it was dealt with. At times, I felt very guilty at being extremely happy and excited at my visit, forgetting that these people's lives had now been turned upside down. Very selfish of me. They were all putting on a brave professional face for the public to which I personally thank them.

As we all entered the prison I could hardly contain myself. We had to go through a procedure of going through some gates which were then closed before opening the other side. I thought this was strange since there were no longer any prisoners in the building, but that is how things were done so I respected that.

We went past some lockers that were put there for the visitors and through an electronic security door, like you see at airports. Then an area where visitors were searched.

There was a small part of floor that was coloured green and I'm afraid my naughty mind thought immediately of the film the Green Mile. We proceeded to a large open room which was the visitors room. The tables all had numbers on them and each table had one red chair for the prisoner and one or sometimes two blue chairs for their visitors to sit on. Placed on the back of each red chair was a sleeveless vest that would have a number on the back that the prisoners would have worn. Cameras were everywhere watching every move. There was a play area in one corner of the room for the young children to keep them occupied. The other end of the room was a refreshment area.

The prisoners would all come out of the same door at one corner of the room and after the visiting hours were over would proceed out through another door at the other corner of the room.

A gentleman named Ian told us the history of the prison first, before our tour. He was an extremely knowledgeable man. We then left the visitors centre to start the tour. Myself and my friend Nic looked at each other with big grins on our faces, even though Nic had worked at the prison briefly before.

We were taken out into a yard were there were buildings for drug rehabilitation and where some prisoners sewed mail bags. Ian said they had to sew precisely 8 stitches to the inch otherwise they would be nicked, as he put it. He also added that they were very good at it and it was a very popular job to do.

Ian also said that the same area, years before, was once a beautiful garden with flowers everywhere and actually won an award for the best kept prison garden in the country. They also grew their own vegetables in a greenhouse there. All now sadly gone and is now just a concrete yard.

We then went through a very large gate where the other side of it were two very big kennels that housed the prison dogs that they used to sniff out drugs.

Darren told me that in this area a prison officer said he heard laughing behind a small wooden fence and wooden gate, yet no one was there.

Ohhh I thought, the first spooky bit.

We then turned a corner alongside the outer prison wall and Ian told us about the three layers of wall that had to be made higher by law.

On the corner was a building called Glevum House, which

was once the Governor's House and in the 60's The Governor moved out and it became the officers mess.

We then went by a building where the prisoners were allowed to have a bath. This is the area were the term 'slopping out' was used. The prisoners were given a bucket which they had to empty out every morning. Eww, no wonder they wanted a bath after. However, the bath water was only supposed to be exactly 8 inches deep. If it was any higher they would be nicked.

We then came to the infamous B wing were Ian pointed out the drop area where prisoners were once hung. This part has now been removed but you can still see the outline of where it was.

Ian said contrary to public belief, all the executions were clean and no one was left dangling, as some people had previously heard.

Opposite the drop was where the bodies were buried. Ian said there is a ledger somewhere where it states who was buried there. But he did not know where it was. He also stated that before a modern part of the building was built over the graves, they were re buried.

We then turned another corner where it was pointed out to us above were four windows separate from the others and marked A2 14, A2 13, A2 12 and A2 11. These four windows connected to the eventual hanging area.

The first two rooms were the daytime rooms where the condemned prisoner was kept and where they were allowed the most daylight.

The second two rooms were the sleeping area. Officers were with them the whole time before their scheduled hanging.

We then went along a little further where it was pointed out to us a trap door that went underground and there was a well there and when Gloucester had the floods, many years ago, this well would fill up.

This trap door was very near where the old prison door was.

We then went into another large area where we were shown on the wall graffiti as far back as the 1800's where prisoners had carved their names in the bricks. Apparently, Fred West had supposedly carved his initials there but no one has yet found it. That gave me a cold shiver.

We then went further along to an area that used to be the main front gate and where this area was they used to hang prisoners from just above the door by Barrack Square end.

On coming back on ourselves, Nicky looked up and saw a bag hanging by some string and asked Darren what it was for. He told her she didn't want to know. I said, "Is it what I am thinking of?" He said "yes, prisoners would go to toilet in it and throw it at the officers as they walked by outside". You can guess what I mean...eww.

Whether they missed one or it was there for us to talk about we didn't know.

Ian told us that there is a tunnel underneath the prison leading to the crown court to take prisoners to the court without having to go outside the walls. It was a very effective way but sadly it was eventually all stopped with no real reason given.

We then went inside A wing. This was what I was waiting for. A massive surge of excitement came over me, here I was going inside the prison and into the cells.

There was a corridor with cells either side then a landing with cells either side again and further up again another landing with more cells either side. There was netting covering the whole area from top to bottom, so no one could jump.

This area my shoulders really started to tingle, my sign that something happened here.

Then Darren pointed out that the landing above the third cell along, number 325, was where the 'ghost' of Jenny Godfrey has been seen. I then knew why I had that tingling feeling. It was creepy.

Also, prison officer Luke Baker told me this was an area that is so very cold at night when he has done a night shift here.

We then crossed over from A wing to B wing where we were allowed to go inside the cells.

Some cells had single beds and some had bunk beds in. All had this blue covered like foam mattresses that felt very hard and with an equally hard headrest. I call it that because that was hard too and not like a pillow.

Each room had a couple of very basic cupboards, a table with a fixed seat, a small wall safe, which I must admit I was surprised to see, a TV a sink and a toilet.

I walked along the corridor and suddenly had a thumping headache outside cell 22. I walked on by and my headache

went as suddenly as it started.
The next cell was number 21. As I walked by it was freezing, and I mean freezing. None of the other cells or anywhere in the whole wing was as cold as this.

Nicky and I asked if we could go in a cell and be locked in for a while. This was granted and we went in cell 23. Ian slammed the door shut and we sat there looking around, then he opened the door. We wanted to stay in there longer, but they had to finish the tour.

Cell 9 was called the safe cell where an inmate was put if needed so they would not harm themselves in any way. There was nothing in that cell they could use to harm themselves. There was a door with hard plastic around it and was shut but an officer would be sat in the corridor right outside the door 24/7 watching out for the prisoner.

We carried on then to an area that we were told was the tray wash area. Officer Luke told me that one night while he was on duty he heard a massive loud crash where he found all the trays on the floor. No one was in there.

We then went into the main exercise yard next to the old prison Chapel. Netting had to be put up all above to cover the main walls where previously, inmate's friends would throw tennis balls over the wall with drugs in. You can imagine the rush to get that ball.

Ian told us another story where pigeons were everywhere before the netting. The inmates would feed them so fat, so they couldn't fly, their friends would catch them outside the prison, kill them and they would be filled with drugs and thrown back over the wall. Since the netting was put up that all stopped. The poor pigeons are now wondering why the food has stopped.

The last place we saw was the closed visiting area where no contact would be made between inmates and visitors. We were then shown out and back to our normal lives.

What an Amazing experience that was.

Hunters Hall

We visited Hunters Hall in 2010 and had a very interesting night.

The Hunters Hall hotel, sits in the Gloucestershire hamlet of Kingscote, only a short distance from Tetbury, Stroud, Nailsworth in the heart of the Cotswolds, with easy access from the A46 and A4135. The earliest record of the Hunters Hall was in 1604 when it comprised a house, an Inn, stables and a Smith's shop. Early in the 20th century, entertainment and dances were held above the stables. Today, the Hunters Hall continues to be a social centre, serving both the local community and travellers. The Hunters Hall has a wealth of charm and character, enhanced by beamed ceilings and open fires. Inside it is still the perfect picture of an old English Inn, with stone-flagged floors, blackened beams, great stone hearths with smoke-darkened oak lintels and ancient cast-iron fire baskets and firebacks, stuffed animals in glass cases, huge wooden settles, shooting prints, old guns on brackets and oak plank tables. It's in a great location for exploring the beautiful Gloucestershire countryside.

While we were there we toured the building, inside and outside in the adjoining grounds. Outside was just as interesting as inside.

Several of us saw strange shadows in the trees and wooded areas, a constant feeling of being watched. Our Medium picked up on a small band of people that use to dwell there, a bit like today's travellers, but made their homes in the woods and made it their own community. I myself saw several unexplained shadows and lots of sparkly lights, as did other people.

I know some of what I write will be picked to pieces by sceptics, but I really don't care to be honest. I know what I saw and felt, and it is truly amazing what we can see and hear if we only use our talent the way it once was used in my opinion. Lost to many because of the pace and lifestyle of today.

When we went inside, there were several little areas and bars to explore and I went into a small bar or snug as it would have been called at one time. I sensed it once was a kitchen and said they may have seen an old lady cooking at an open fire with big black open pots. This was confirmed to me by staff. No one had previously told us anything before we arrived.

We also picked up on a priest hole that was used in the back and top of the fireplace. I went to have a look and fell back just as if someone had given me an almighty push. Luckily someone caught me before I nearly crashed to the floor. Not disheartened, I had another look as I was extremely intrigued. Again, on looking up the chimney, I fell back and was very dizzy and felt sick, which wasn't from looking up, it was not that kind of feeling, it was more than that. Someone was up there and did not want to be found.

Our Medium confirmed it was a priest and he was terrified at being found and was shouting and pushing me to get away.

I did not chance a third time. Would you have done? Yeh Right! I know it's easy to say 'yeh I would' but it's a lot different when you are there. The feelings, the sense of fear, the sheer adrenaline taking over, just to satisfy your thirst for the 'spooky unexplained'.
So many times, when people come on our overnight investigations really are very frustrated because they desperately want to see or hear something.

What's that saying? Be careful what you wish for.

Lilly's Restaurant & Tea room

Psychic medium and friend of mine Lorna Hedges introduced me to Tania Meecham, manageress of Lilly's Restaurant in College Court, Gloucester in December 2010. A very quaint and rather busy restaurant tucked away in the corner of the old medieval wall that runs along the side of the restaurant and very popular with tourists and local people.

Not knowing anything about the history of this building, I was soon to find out how much ghostly activity has been, and still is, going on there.

On one of Lorna's visits in the Spring of 2010, she went out the back to have a look and was shocked when the door was slammed in her face, yet no one was there.

Tania told us of a customer that was having a meal in the restaurant. He had picked up his knife and fork and they were being pulled out of his hands by force. He was left visibly shaken by his ordeal and went very pale, reported Tania.

On another occasion, a rather large heavy coffee machine was pushed off the counter right in front of the staff and customers.

In a small corner from time to time, there is a very pungent smell at the same time as a man has been seen, rather oddly dressed sitting there. Then it and he, disappeared.

Tania has agreed for our paranormal team to investigate what exactly is going on there. Very soon I hope.

The spirit children of Woodchester Mansion
by my dear friend and fellow author, Martin.R.Gillott

Having been interested in the world of spirit for some time now, I have been lucky enough to experience several unexplained happenings.
The one that intrigued me most is, in my opinion, still ongoing as you will see.

I have visited Woodchester Mansion four times now and on my first all night investigation, I was with several people in the area of the kitchen when I suddenly felt a slight brush on my right cheek. I reported to Lyn at once what had happened and on further investigation it was discovered that I had received a scratch.

I had been aware that there were spirit children around us as several of our group had mentioned their own experiences on that vigil and felt it to be them who had scratched me. Further on in that vigil it was to happen for a second time, this time on my forehead.

A few weeks later I was back there and the same thing happened in exactly the same spot, one on my forehead and one on my cheek. Why was I being singled out? Having given this a lot of thought over the next few weeks, it suddenly dawned on me that I was the only person there that had been wearing a hearing aid. Perhaps that was it. So, on my next visit I decided to take out my hearing aid and to enter the area of the kitchen without it. And yes, you've guessed it, no scratches. However, we visited that area again later and with hearing aid in place I received yet another scratch.

Upon returning home I immediately contacted a colleague of mine who is a specialist in the field of hearing problems. We both came up with the theory that as this particular piece of apparatus is prone to whistling at certain times (feedback) which, if we can hear it then it is possible that it may well give off a noise that is out of our sensory range but may well be within the range of spirit. I have known in the past were high pitched noises were used in order to contact the other side.

On my last visit, I gave it one more go and came away with two scratches, only this time they were to draw blood.
I am going back there in a month and this time I will be ready. I shall wear padded gloves taped onto my wrists and have my hands held by a person on each side of me. If the same thing occurs then I shall be convinced that the spirits are involved. Okay, it may not convince everyone but I am not in the business of doing that. I leave that to others who are cleverer than me. I will at least rule out that I may be inflicting scratches on myself subconsciously, which I can't imagine doing but I am informed that it is possible.

Only then can I put my hand on my heart and say that I have been of interest to the spirit children that roam the kitchen of Woodchester Mansion.

The next story concerns bishop Hooper's lodgings, the folk museum, in Westgate street. My mum (Phyllis Phelps) worked there for many years, usually in the mornings, but sometimes in the afternoon. If she worked in the afternoon, I would go there after school. One afternoon I was in the room reputedly where bishop Hooper spent his last night. On the wall was a cabinet with lockable doors, and inside was a script relating to bishop Hooper. The doors were opened in the day and locked at night. It was an overcast day with no wind and suddenly, very slowly, the cabinet doors started to close. I was amazed so much that I watched them close, then I realized what I had seen and ran. I went down to tell my mum and the other lady who was working. They said they had seen it happen before.

Also, they told me on many occasions they had heard someone call them only to find the place empty. And apparently many times the kettle in the kitchen would be hot when they unlocked in the morning. Plus, they said there were always unexplained noises, and temperatures would drop suddenly.

I did an investigation at the museum several years ago with some friends and we found the museum very spooky, especially at night and in the attic room. We were all sitting very quiet in the upstairs room where the old machines were when we all heard footsteps coming along the corridor just below us. Expecting to see some more of our colleagues, we waited but no one came. It was as if the footsteps stopped suddenly at the end of the corridor with stairs leading up to where we were all sitting. Very strange indeed. We asked the other team that was in another part of the building well away from us if it was any of them. They all said no it was not any of them but when they were in the upstairs room where we were, they said they heard the same thing and thought it was us. But It wasn't. Can two groups of people both be wrong?

Mary Phelps January 10, 2011 at 11:14 pm

Hi lyn. The first story was told to me by my grandmother, who was a very good Christian woman who would lie. My grandmother (Ada French) was fire watching with a friend Miss Morgan, at the cathedral during world war two. It was apparently a cold evening and they were in the cloisters. My gran decided to go and get some hassocks from the choir stalls to sit on. As she got to the choir stalls, she saw a monk. He passed her about 18 inches away. He went to the altar rail, knelt down and disappeared. She said she wasn't at all afraid. The following day she mentioned it to the dean who told her he had been sighted several times, and they felt he was concerned about the stained-glass window, and decided to remove it until the war was over.

I have purposely included some history of this next building, as I feel it will appeal to people outside of Gloucester and all over the world that are interested in old historic buildings and would not usually be privy to such detailed information.

Gloucester, Southgate St, Robert Raikes' House

Merchant's house, later shop and dwelling, now shop (No.36) and public house (The Golden Cross, No.38). Mid to late C16 with substantial early C18 addition at rear and internal alterations; C19 and C20 alterations. Timber frame with wattle and daub panels, brick, slate roof, two brick stacks with octagonal shafts. PLAN: a block comprising two, lateral, timber-framed ranges of three bays with a third, parallel range and a cross wing both in brick added at rear in early C18, the northern bay converted to shop and dwelling and the central and southern bays converted to public house with staff accommodation in the upper floors.

EXTERIOR: three storeys, attic and cellars; on the front three cross-gabled bays jettied at first, second and attic floor levels; on the ground floor a late C20 shop-front to No.36, a mid C20 front to the barroom of the public house has large windows with glazing bars between the timber storey posts. The upper floors a good example of West Country decorative timber framing: a similar pattern to both upper floors, in each bay divided into three by secondary posts and into three horizontal zones of small panels, with ogee braces in the lower panels, quadrant braces in the angles of the intermediate panels and plain upper panels; in each of the attic cross gables a lower zone of small panels with quadrant braces in the angles. The framing pattern, probably painted, is repeated on the return end walls of the range at second-floor level. The first-floor jetty is supported by consoles and the second and attic floors by curved knee braces off the storey posts with moulded bressumers above. The gables have scalloped and pierced barge boards and turned spike finials.

On both of the upper floors in each end bay a central C19 horned sash and in the central bay a similar sash to either side of central panels of framing; in each gable a small pair of casements above the zone of panels. Rear elevation of two storeys and attic; four bays with a single bay return end to right; raised band at first-floor level and crowning modillion cornice. Doorway in second bay from left in a former window opening; replacement early C19 sashes to ground floor with slender glazing bars (3x4 panes) and original sashes to first floor with thick glazing bars (3x5 panes); four gabled roof dormers each with a pair of casements. HISTORY: The Gloucester Journal was first published from 36/38 Southgate Street by Robert Raikes Senior on 9th April, 1722. Raikes moved his printing office here in 1758, transferring it from Blackfriars. A notable example of a later C16 town house, with ornamental panelling in the West Midlands carpentry tradition.

Many of the house's original features remain. It's been one of the biggest refurbishment projects Gloucester has ever seen. Robert Raikes' House in Gloucester has reopened after a two year refurbishment project. The 16th century building is now a pub, named after a former resident. Robert Raikes was the man behind Sunday Schools.

The building has a rich history having been a pub, private house and shop. The first Sunday Schools were held in the garden of the building on Gloucester's Southgate Street.

Sue And Phil Tandy used to run this fabulous renovated house, but sadly have now moved away.
Sue confirmed to me recently that she too had felt, on several occasions, that some unknown presence was with her in the kitchen and around the area that I had previously seen myself and documented in my first book, Paranormal Gloucester.

Sue said she was too afraid to say anything in case people thought she was crazy, but on reading my book she decided to tell me, and very glad I am too, as I can now verify it was not just me.

Sue also told me that one night, around 2am after service, her and Phil were chilling out after a busy night with a glass of wine, and just chatting in the bar. No one else was with them, it was all locked up.

Suddenly, they both heard heavy foot or boots steps directly above them, walking along the floor. They both looked at each other and was quite startled, both saying at the same time, "Did you hear that?" They both agreed they had heard it and did not know what to make of it. The above rooms are only accessible with a key that Sue and Phil do not give out to anyone. And at the top of the stairs, the upper floors are derelict and empty. Phil did quip and said to Sue, "Please don't tell Lyn, she will have a field day". But I am glad to say she did. Phil says he does not believe in ghosts yet he said he cannot explain some of the strange things that happen there.

This story is told by Hannah Jarvie, who worked at the Robert Raikes House

The first thing that happened was in the kitchen whilst I was cutting up some carrots. There were some ramekins on the back of the shelf and for some reason, one of them flew off the shelf and smashed at the back of my feet, for no apparent reason.

The next incident was when they were closing down the pub one evening and they both heard breathing and footsteps, yet they knew all the customers had left the building. They still decided to double check every room which were completely empty.

The third incident I experienced was when I assumed someone was in the downstairs disabled toilet (incidentally right next to the kitchen). I was talking away, thinking it was my partner. The handrail had been turned on and I tried the door and it was locked and my partner was not in there.

The fourth thing that happened was when me and my boyfriend went upstairs into the upper empty floors to look around. It was more what we felt than saw as we both felt we were being watched and followed the whole time they were up there. We were drawn to a few rooms where we felt cold spots and felt goose bumps when we walked past a few places.

Another time, in the bar, witnessed by the Landlord Phil and a few customers, all saw where they put the empty glasses into a tray to be washed and one glass just appeared to come straight up out of the tray and smashed onto the floor and into the glass washer where Phil had to clean it all out in case any pieces of glass were still in there. No one was near the glass.

Hannah's partner Ben Portman, also verified that he had seen a black dog and heard him pitter patter along the stone floor in the corridor quite a few times, again previously noted in my first book.

One of the rooms, just off the corridor entrance, are some really nice large comfy seats with high backs to them. When I first went into this room after the pub had just opened, I was immediately drawn to this one particular chair in the corner of the room and sat down. This is the very same chair Ben and Hannah described to me that they have both seen, out of the corner of their eye, a figure of a man sat there. Yet on looking straight at the chair no one was sitting there.

Several times as they walked past they had seen this figure but he quickly disappears.

Ben and Hannah say most occurrences happen after they have closed down. They both have said that they do not feel anything nasty around the pub, but in one of the very top rooms not used, they said they feel that there is a nasty presence there and will not go up there on their own. Stewart Cook, a customer at The Robert Raikes house, has told me that he is a sceptic but around late November 2010, he was visiting the gentleman's toilets upstairs in the pub. It was a quiet night and including himself there were only about 6 people in there. As he was coming towards the door after being in the gents, he heard four heavy footsteps outside in the corridor. He expected to see the door open and a male come in, but no one did, so he opened the door and looked in the corridor, yet there was no one about. He went down stairs, back to the bar, and no one else had moved. They were all accounted for, and no one else had come in to the pub. He thought it was very strange as he was very adamant he heard these footsteps and yet no one was there in the corridor.

This is the same area that women have reported not liking and a feeling of being watched. Even in the ladies they have said they feel very uncomfortable in there.

Vicky Mcculloch's story
Robinhood Street, Gloucester

When I was a kid, my mum kept hearing footsteps up and down the stairs. This went on for ages. She shouted up the stairs one day "I'm not scared. I know there is someone there". Something bolted the stairs door from the inside.

My sister had to squeeze through a tiny little window and come down the stairs to open the door. She was so scared she said she felt like a presence was there. She felt like someone was sat on her bed one day, and would never go in the back bedroom again. Lots of things happened in the house. My mum still lives there now.

Myself, my dad and my sister also saw a white orb that just made you stare at it. So weird.

St. James Club. Gloucester

Psychic medium Lorna Hedges told me this story and I have to say, I was very Interested and surprised on hearing it, as I never realized this had happened or indeed why.

Upstairs in a back room, apparently a man shouts and bawls at people for no apparent reason, and has done from time to time.

A customer went in to the toilets one night, and as he came out, someone was leaning over the banister shouting at him. When he asked about this man in the bar, they said "What man? No one lives upstairs and no one is up there right now." But then told him of the story.

What makes me wonder is, it isn't always the ghost or spirit of that particular place, but a previous place or area, and this is where the research comes in to it.

Fascinating and very time consuming, but well worth the effort if you can find out the history of who lived, worked, or died there before.

Tracy Blicks story

Hi Lyn, I had a strange experience when I was working in the antique centre. I was unlocking in the morning so there was nobody else there and nobody could have got in, but as I unlocked the fire escape, I turned and there was a woman looking straight at me through the door. Weird thing is, another lady who works there claims she saw someone on the fire escape the day before and we both described the same woman, even though we haven't spoken to each other. There's definitely something there though, because the furniture moves at night when the rooms are locked up and come the next morning, you can't get in because it's in front of the door. The lady who runs the coffee shop claims she's had stuff thrown at her as well.

Landlady of The Plough Inn. High St Tredworth Gloucester

I hear sounds of what seems like a child running very fast, or it might be a dog running very fast steps, down in the bar. I don't feel so uneasy there but upstairs I do, especially towards the back end of the house, which is mostly empty where we don't go very often. This is the older part of the house. There are five bedrooms up there.

As it's an old building, she puts the noises down to that as it creaks and groans as it heats up and cools down. Yes, it could be, but is it though?

My partner got up in the morning at about 4am to go to work.

He was pulling out of his parking space and something made him look up at the landing window and he saw what he presumed was a child, because he could only see a head and a hand waving at him. He shot off down the road and said it did frighten him. Usually nothing does but this did.

At night, the Cd player and the till are always turned off at the plugs, yet when I got to the bottom door I could hear music, and I knew I was the only one there. It was the stereo and the till, the two things that are never left on.

Debbie said, "This might sound daft but we left a lollipop on the side one night, in a certain position. Doreen our bar lady came in the next morning and the lollipop had turned around the other way". She said she doesn't know why, but it all points to a child, and the name Elizabeth keeps coming into her head.

Three of us have sat many times in the bar area at night and heard keys jangling, and what sounds like a coin dropping on the floor in the kitchen area, yet no one was out there.

All these events happened within a month. April 2009.

Claudette's story

Claudette works at the Plough and says she has had her trousers pulled back several times. She has had glasses in her hand in front of customers and they suddenly shattered, yet have never cut anyone. She has also heard her name being called. She feels it's a man's voice and has felt breathing on her neck, and also had her bra strap flicked quite a bit.

Debbie said the last landlady and her mother had experiences which she was told of and feels there is something in the cellar. She feels it is a man and has named him Charlie. The guy who painted the pub, who doesn't believe in ghosts, said that in the cellar while painting, he felt someone was behind him, so he called out and said, "If that's you Charlie and you want this pub to reopen, you better move on", or words to that effect. With that, he said it felt warm again and got on with the painting.

Debbie's Auntie Marianne stayed there and was talking with Debbie about things in general and the topic got onto ghosts. Marianne said she saw a man's figure standing at the bottom of her bed and he frightened her to death. She said she hadn't really been to sleep. Then to my horror she described what he had on. The colour drained from me as she said, "What is the matter with you?" I went upstairs and got a photograph of a landlady and landlord who had the pub in 1812. I showed it to Marianne, and she said, "That's the man I saw stood at the end of my bed." Waistcoat, gold watch etc. and that is exactly how he looks in the picture.

Another friend Rachel, has had her feet tickled and the blankets pulled off her. Claudette said she stopped at the pub one night and shared the same bed as Rachel, when a heavy quilt was ripped off them and their feet tickled. She added that it was never anything sinister but just played about with their feet.

Out the back of the pub, Claudette said she feels like someone is walking heavy footed past her, and she feels this quite frequently. She has deliberately stayed still to see what happened. When she has walked into the bar and no one else is in there with her she says she can feel the movement of someone on the suspended floor.

Most of these occurrences happen at night, but also certain things still happen in the day. When she has seen people walk through the same wall, yet when she turns around, there is no one there. It's mostly corner of the eye stuff she says.
Also, she sees lots of blue or white lights going around the bar and around an area where a jukebox used to be by the wall.

Debbie said that two customers Barry and Heather, thought they saw Debbie walking through the bar into her private quarters one day, but she was out shopping. When she returned they asked her if she had come in five minutes earlier. She said "No, I have only just got back from shopping". They both swore they saw her come in another way five minutes earlier.

Doreen, who works behind the bar, has had her bottom felt more than once. And not by the customers she added.

James, who lives in the pub, said he was in the bathroom one evening leaning over the sink and someone was tickling the bottom of his back. Yet no one was there when he turned around. Another night he was lying in bed and out of the corner of his eye he saw a figure walk past his door, straight into his room and carried on going through the wall.

James, Debbie and Claudette were in the kitchen one time when Claudette walked out and heard like a sigh. They both stood there and heard it at the same time. They both looked at each other, each thinking the other had sighed. They went looking for Claudette but she was nowhere near them. Whatever it was, was right between them, and it was that near

Debbie said she felt as if someone had breathed directly on her face.

Debbie said she got a dog. She's only 14 weeks old and James was giving her a guided tour of the pub. They went in several rooms without any trouble, but when it came to a room at the start of a corridor, she refused to go in there and just sat down and howled. Debbie explained to us it was just an empty bedroom so couldn't understand why the dog howled.

April 7th, 2009, I did a walk around the Plough Inn with Debbie, James and Claudette and one room in particular I was rather drawn to. It was at the front of the house facing the road into High Street. I felt compelled to sit in a chair in the corner of the room, and had a feeling this was once a living room belonging to a lady called Betty. Then I saw in my mind's eye, elvers and ladies standing outside gossiping. This was Betty's home. She would have scrubbed her own steps, and was very particular in her housework in her home. I contacted her on her own. I got that her husband died in the army, Robinswood Barracks came into my head also which is not that far away from the pub. Trevor was her son. My dictaphone was acting up at this point. Then I took some pictures in the room.

Betty had a large family, mostly sons. She wore little slippers that she shuffled around the house in.

All of which I cannot 100% verify until I do some research on past residents of this building. So who knows what else or who else resides in the pub as well as the landlord and lady.

A story that has happened to me personally
May 27th, 2011; Woodchester Mansion

I have had many experiences at Woodchester Mansion, but none so amazing as this night. I had a strong feeling that the night was going to be good, but never envisaged it to be happening to myself.

I was called to assist in the upstairs bathroom where several people were doing a glass board session, when they encountered a lady spirit that was asking for help. So someone came to fetch me. I went upstairs to find they had asked the lady if 'lyn' (myself) was to help her. The glass indicated yes.

I said, "What did she want exactly?"
They said, "We think she wants to cross over".
I said I had never done that before and "Why me? I am not qualified to do this." They were very adamant that I was the one to help this lady.

So I asked a colleague to fetch the Ouija Board so that we could gain more information.
The lady spelt out her name 'Elizabeth'. She was still looking for her son who had drowned in the lake. His name was Adrian. She was 19, he was 6 years old.

I sat at the table, still not convinced I could help, but felt I had to try. I became very emotional and said a prayer and with a lot of love and respect I asked my Spirit Guides to come forward and help, and for Angels to collect this lady and reunite her with her son.

Everyone in the room said they felt it was right and felt I had helped her, each one having a strange feeling or a feeling of joy that she had gone and was now with her son.

My colleague Dave Mason, said he felt a cold breeze go right across his arm towards the window, which he said felt odd as he thought a breeze would come from the window not go to the window.

I got quite emotional and had a tear or two, as did a couple of other people in the room. I still wondered if I did the right thing, and it was not an ego thing. Also, who did I think I was? Did I have the right to do that?

All I know is it did feel right. I prayed from the heart and only hope Elizabeth and Adrian are together again.

Earlier on in the evening, everybody was in the kitchen and corridor leading into the kitchen. We did our usual calling out, and had a few odd feelings that the 'nasty' man was with us, but he wasn't playing on our terms. He would do what he wanted to do in his own time. Apparently, he does not like the ladies and enjoys frightening them. Several people said they were getting very strong drafts going past them and at the back of them, icy cold drafts. We also kept smelling a very strong smell of beer, yet no one had drunk any beer. Towards the end of the kitchen vigil, I saw in my mind's eye a tall man in a tall black top hat and long cape. He had a black cane under his arm and was crouching down as he walked.

Helen, the lady that was taking care of us, said I described him to a tee. Yet I had never seen him before or had been told about him. So that was well spooky. The same time as I was describing him, my colleague Dave and another person saw the same man at the end of the front corridor.

They did not know I was describing him to Helen, and I didn't know they had just seen him, until we spoke afterwards.
This sort of information is very interesting, especially when verified by more than one person and without any prior knowledge.

G.A.P.S account of Woodchester Mansion

Since G.A.P.S has been formed in 2010, we have been to Woodchester Mansion several times. Here are some of our experiences there to date.

Rhonda Lane's story

I can think of the spirit of the crying woman in the ladies' toilets, the "shadow" dog-which may have been the reason for my fall that time and the orb photo I got in the chapel. I took two pictures, one after the other, and in the second picture there is an orb in the right upper side of the window, which seems to have something in it. When we were doing the circle, I felt like somebody was behind me and took two pictures. The first one had so many orbs it was like a 3D effect, but the second picture, taken right after, didn't have a single orb. Both pictures were taken over my shoulder. I didn't turn, so it wasn't dust kicked up. Before I took the pictures, like I said, I felt like someone was behind me, and I then felt someone link their arm in mine. The girl next to me that I was holding hands with in the circle remarked how cold my arm had gone, so she picked up on it too.

David and I did a vigil and tried to record in the ladies' toilets. We didn't hear her crying on his recording, but we did get a dog barking and what sounded like someone whistling, as if they were calling the dog to them. But I remember walking into the ladies that one night and a girl was standing outside a stall asking, "Are you alright? Did something happen? Do you want me to get somebody?" The crying was loud enough to be heard outside. The girl standing outside the cubicle asked if I could help, so I started talking, telling whoever, that I was with the team and could help her, but no answer. I looked down and saw no feet or legs, and that's when I knew nobody was in there. So, I looked over the stall (my heart was racing, I literally had no idea what I might see or would happen!) and nobody was there. And the crying, which distinctly came from there, stopped. When they put in the new toilets, I wondered if the crying lady would still be around. Instead, it felt oppressive and threatening in the ladies. I don't scare easy, but I really didn't like it. I dreaded it. I asked a few of the guys if they had the same feeling in the men's, and they said no.

Helen Adair's story, 20th February at 20:09

Carol Beasmore and I have visited Woodchester for overnight vigils on two occasions now. During my first visit, we were sat with a small group in the room which was used as a morgue. Something encouraged me to venture out into the corridor. I can't explain that but I know the feeling was quite strong, and I was drawn to the corridor by the front door (the one we usually enter the building in). I stood there for a little while and then very unexpectedly burst into tears, I mean real sobbing, which took me very much by surprise. On this occasion, my friends ushered me back to the control room where we informed Lyn of the incident.

During my second visit, Carol and I first ventured down to the cellars where someone sensed there were children spirits present. All of a sudden, we smelt 'old fashioned' perfume and again, I burst into tears for no apparent reason. However, on this occasion I sensed the spirit of a woman and for some reason, the name Elizabeth.

Later that same evening, Lyn planned to do a vigil in the kitchen to attempt to summon a more malevolent spirit which Lyn had encountered on her previous visit to Woodchester. Carol, myself and a young couple asked if we could go down to the kitchen before everyone else and Lyn agreed but emphasized to us that everyone else would remain in the control room and no one would be wandering around. We sat in the dark and all experienced an odd arc shaped light in the left hand corner of the room and strange intermittent whistling!

If you remember Lyn, you all joined us and about 10 of us formed a circle. A little while later, as I started to cry again, a few of us, Carol included, smelt a sweet, flowery perfume, the same as earlier that evening but much stronger this time and I sensed the same lady spirit touch me twice on the head. I am most definitely certain about this! I think you offered her the light but I am certain she wanted to stay. I felt as though she was looking for someone, possibly a child, and this may explain the overwhelming grief I seem to experience when she was in our presence.

After my experience, I received spiritual healing as I was exhausted, and then followed yourself up to the same corridor I first encountered the lady, by the front door. If you remember, you were stood up the far end of the corridor, I was positioned half way down where I know I was stood in the first instance. I know I should have, but I didn't mention this to anyone. She came to me again, the same perfume, but didn't stay long.

Do you think this was because the healer had placed a protection circle around me?

Emma Pemberton's story, 20th February

I'll never forget my very first trip to Woodchester. The atmosphere was amazing and it was a clear, crisp Autumnal evening. I used to smoke back then and I would often take time in the breaks to go out the back door for a quick cigarette or to visit the ladies, which was situated in a port-a-cabin in the car park. Well, every time I walked toward the back door it had this weird way of opening. At first, I didn't notice but then mom and my friends commented that the door would open for me. As if I had my own imaginary butler, but never on the way in, only the way out. It happened every single time I went out that night, but not when a friend tried to walk in front of me. Sadly, my butler appears to have only been in residence for one night only as it's not happened since. I have to admit I kind of liked it.

It was one very, very cold February night and CEP had done an investigation there in conduction with IOPR. The evening had gone quite well. We had a few things, and then a small group of us had gone to the bathroom. Fortunately, I had the foresight to put the dictaphone on the mantle piece, when as I stood by the door way, I clearly heard very faint sounds of Gregorian Chanting. It would then fade out and come back again, and I have to be honest, it didn't sound as if it was coming from our time, if you know what I mean. Now I never, ever thought that the dictaphone would in a million years pick this up, but you know what? It did. How fantastic was that! I can tell you it quite threw me.

Annette Pemberton, February 22nd, 2011

This also occurred in the same room, the bathroom. My friend Alison and I had gone into this room on our own. I had sat with my back to the window facing the door. Alison had started pacing up and down and acting slightly aggressive, which kind of worried me a bit. The room at the time felt as if an uneasy presence was there, but then it changed and it stopped. I thought nothing more about it, but as I do with every investigation, I had my dictaphone on, and I always write up a report and take picture and then listen to hours of dictaphone. I was sat with my headphones on in my office in the dark, when suddenly and very clearly at this point, you can hear a man shout at both of us to get out. Now I know that we didn't hear that in the room at that time and I would have run like hell. It made me jump so much hubby came running up the stairs, at this point wondering what the hell had happened.

My friend Mike and I decided to go ghost hunting a few years ago. Mike really wanted to go to the Ram Inn in Wotton Under Edge and take some photos. Sadly, all I had with me at the time was my mobile phone camera. When we arrived at the Ram Inn, John gave us a tour. We went into the area where people would sit and drink. I decided to get a photo of "The Ancient Grave". Later on, I copied the photo to my pc so I could get a better look at the photo and I found a face on the floor just to the right of the grave. On another visit to the Ram Inn, Mike and I arrived at the same time as another bloke and his wife. After a short chat, John called us and allowed us in. This bloke's wife point blank refused to enter the building and waited outside. John opened the attic but due to the condition of the staircase, Mike and this bloke refused to go up so I went on my own. Although I didn't get anything on camera, I did feel as though I wasn't wanted in there and that feeling wasn't coming from John. He was engaged in a conversation with Mike and this bloke.

On another ghost hunt, Mike and I decided to go to Littledean Jail. Mike asked me to take a photo of the "SPOOKY" sign in the cell block, so I did. Again, I copied the photo to my pc. As I zoomed in on the photo, I noticed a tiny amount of mist. I decided to zoom into it a bit more and found a very faint face in the mist.

Another hunt included a trip to Devil's Chapel, which is just woodland now. From what I have been told, it used to be some sort of mine. It has caved in and is now just woodland. I was standing on a track and felt something on my back. I mentioned it to Mike and he looked at my back straight away. He said, "Your coats pushed in". I handed him my camera and asked him to take a photo. The photo shows 2 orbs and a hand print on my back. I felt it on my back until I left the woodland and got back to the main road.

The Ram Inn story: Karen Tury, Becky Toomey And Charlotte Toomey, February 21st, 2012

The girls went into the driveway of the Ram Inn just looking around as they had heard so much about this place in the media. They decided to take some pictures, but Becky suddenly felt very light headed and didn't feel right at all, so she decided to get back into the car. The other girls followed her.

They were all sat in the car for about 10 to 15 minutes then Karen wanted to get back out. She was filming around the drive when she heard a deep husky voice that told her to get out. This was coming from her left side. She chose to ignore this and carried on filming. When she had finished, she got back into the car, and immediately felt pins and needles in her right arm and had a very heavy banging headache.

She was listening and talking to her friends about the audio on her camcorder and within 2 minutes of watching it, Becky became light headed and saw a white flash across her eyes. Then the white turned into a black circle and coming through the black circle, she saw red eyes which then formed into a male's face. She said it was an old face with deep scars and lines. Then it formed into a full-bodied apparition of a tall dark outline of a man.

They decided to leave the car park and drove up the road about a mile and nearly crashed into another car from sheer panic. So, they pulled off the road to calm down and to ring their friend Kim Barnes, to explain what had happened. Kim invited them round to her house where she said a protection prayer.

They were talking about the incident when suddenly, they all looked at Karen's arm. It was all red and very tender to touch. She could not explain how this had happened.

They stayed about an hour with Kim then went home. Karen says she had a restless night, so she had a shower and then noticed all her arm was bruised. She took some pictures of it, and then felt sick and had a headache. An experience she will never forget.

Trish Benness: 25th December

Even though I was still married to my first husband, I will refer to him as ex-husband.

My ex-husband wanted to go see one of his friends and have a few drinks, therefore I was expected to go with him and then drive home.
As soon as we got to the house, which I had never visited before, I felt uncomfortable. I just put it down to the fact that I'd never been there before and I didn't particularly like my ex's friend. But that uncomfortable feeling grew increasingly as I entered the house and sat down in the lounge, while my ex went into the study with his friend.

I was left in the lounge with my ex's friend's wife and kids. Who, again, I didn't really get along with as we had absolutely nothing in common. I started to actually feel quite, sick, is the only word I can think of, although not physically sick, it's really hard to explain. I moved seats because I thought I was too close to the heater, but that made me feel 10 times worse. I really needed to get some air as I felt I couldn't breathe, like something was literally clinging to my chest.

I told my ex I was just going to sit in the car for a bit and to come out when he was ready as I was starting to fall asleep and needed fresh air to wake me up. No way could I tell him about this 'feeling', he would just get angry at having to leave early.

I went out and sat on the kerb but still felt like I'd been sat on. I actually felt drained and like I could sleep for a day. My ex came out about 15 minutes later and we went home. Although I felt like I could sleep the instant my head hit the pillow, I couldn't get to sleep. I kept having this feeling that I'd forgotten to do something. Something really important. But for the life of me couldn't think what.

I ignored the feeling for a while but it kept getting stronger and stronger and after about 2 weeks of little or no sleep each night, I started to think on what it could be. All of a sudden, I saw an image of a little girl of about 1 year old, and I heard her whisper 'daddy'. I can't tell you if it was an image in my head or actually in front of me because when I shut my eyes I could still see her.

Every night she would 'visit', where I could see her and she would whisper 'daddy'. But during the day I couldn't see her, it was only a feeling that she was with me because I had that 'clinging' feeling again around my chest, but not so tight anymore. I started to get the feeling that I was actually carrying her and she had her legs around my waist and arms around my neck.

I thought maybe it was my 'maternal clock' letting me know that my time was running out to have kids, but put that away as I never planned on having kids, especially with my ex.

This went on for about 2 months. I was absolutely drained and when my ex asked me one day what was wrong with me, I finally told him everything. He is a believer in ghosts and spirits as well so was really amazed that I'd had such an experience, and told me I can't just deny something like that and go with it to see what happens. Which really shocked me, I thought he'd just tell me to forget her and move on.

We both got invited to a bbq at his friend's house and I told my ex to tell them I couldn't go as I didn't feel well. I didn't want that suffocating feeling again.

My ex had had a few to drink with his friend and they were talking about houses, as my ex and I were looking to build or buy our first home. His friend said they were thinking about selling but couldn't make the final decision whether to sell or not. My ex asked if anyone had lived in the house before them. His friend said no, they had built the house, as they had decided to start a family and needed more than a 2-bedroomed unit because they wanted 2 girls and 2 boys. They were nearly there, they had the 2 boys and only 1 girl. My ex for some strange reason (that only alcohol and he knows) blurted out why I really wasn't there. He said his friend went white as a sheet and literally fell backwards into a chair and started crying!

After some time, my ex's friend told him that they actually had 2 girls and 2 boys but one of the girls had died due to illness very young and that sometimes he felt her still in the house which is why they couldn't decide to move or not. He said sometimes he'd be sitting at his desk and everyone else was asleep he said he sometimes thought he heard a girl calling 'daddy' so he'd turn around thinking his little girl who should be sleeping was there but she wasn't. He'd then check on her and she'd be sound asleep in her bed.

My ex came home and told me this and I felt that really tight clinging feeling again and that feeling of having forgotten something really important, but this time I didn't panic. I 'listened'. I told my ex to tell his friend she just wants to tell her daddy that she's ok and not sick anymore and it's ok for them to move if they want to.

A few weeks later, my ex's friend personally told me thank you and that they had now made the decision to move. He never told his wife about any of this because she still hadn't gotten over the loss of her first daughter, her first child.

Once I had passed on the message to my ex's friend, I never felt or saw her again. I felt the loss almost physically because I had gotten so used to 'carrying' her around with me. But I felt like I had done what I was supposed to do so I let her go in peace.

I have had many experiences prior to and since this but this was the first time I had actually been 'asked' to do something so significant.

Trish Benness, January 10, 2011

In Walhalla (an old gold mining town in Victoria) there is only a population of about 10 people and is literally in the valley of mountains. One way in one way out, one general store, one bakery, one post office. That's is. The nearest big town was over an hour drive. My ex in-laws moved there as it was quiet and peaceful. They were in charge of the now disused gold mine and took tourists in there and told the story about Walhalla. Well, they thought it was peaceful!! I struggled when I was there as there are so many spirits wandering around I was overwhelmed, especially in the gold mine. If I had to take tourists in there that were running late for the tour, I'd end up running out with the feeling of being followed. I'd had a fight with my ex and so I slept in the car one night and boy was that a silly thing to do. There was so much activity. Anyway, there is a grave with a curse on the headstone. No one really knew why, but the man buried there, James Mitchell, had cursed anyone that leaned over his grave to die as quickly as he did. His graveside was the only one that had

a fence around it too. This fascinated me, since I thought maybe it was put there in case anyone accidentally leaned over to read the headstone. The inscription was this:
> 'Oh let my sudden doom
> a warning be to all
> ere whilst thou bendest over my tomb
> thou may as quickly fall'

I contacted births/deaths/marriages registry here in Victoria and tried to find out who he was. All they could tell me was his death was marked suspicious and was never resolved. I did some more investigating and found that he was a food carrier to the miners and on leaving the mine after meals were delivered, he was struck by a 'falling' rock on the head. He lived long enough to dictate to his mum what he wanted on his headstone, which was the 'curse'.

Every time I went to Walhalla I was drawn to James' grave and would just visit with him. I found out after many visits, that he was actually hit over the head by a rock by an angry miner who wanted more food than his ration. Another miner had died and so this miner wanted the food that had been rationed to the dead man. James had told him no because if anyone found out he would lose his job and jobs were so hard to get in those days. Well he didn't just lose his job, he lost his life. The last time I went up to his grave it felt more peaceful than any other time that I had visited him. I guess he just needed someone to know.

Some encounters with the supernatural
By Robert Snow

I consider myself fortunate in as much, that so far in my life, I have had some experiences for which I can find no normal explanation. Therefore, I must call them supernatural or paranormal.

I suppose my first experience of any consequence happened in Dorset in the early sixties. You see as a child, my parents, my sister and me lived in The National provincial Bank House, now The National Westminster Bank, at a small Dorset market town, my father being a bank employee.

Around 1956, if my memory serves me correctly, we moved to Southsea as my father was transferred to a branch of the bank at Portsmouth, but every Christmas we would all return to the Dorset town to stay with some friends who lived in the old rectory. The house is now called 'Bleak House' (name changed to avoid embarrassment to the present owners).

When we visited 'Bleak House' I used to sleep in a room that was known as the sewing room. It was located on a mezzanine floor, halfway between the ground floor and the first floor. The main staircase went from the entrance floor up one flight, at the top of which was the sewing room on the left. There was a ninety degree turn to the right and another flight went up to the first floor.

One particular night in 1960 at Christmas time, I think it was the night of Christmas Eve, but it could have been a couple of days after Christmas. Anyway, I had just finished reading in bed and went over to the door to switch off the overhead light as there was no bedside lamp. I climbed back into bed and lay there with my eyes open with nothing particular on my mind; just looking at the ceiling which was illuminated by the strong moonlight shining through the window which looked into the churchyard.

After a few minutes, I noticed what I can only describe as a circular misty cloud forming over the foot of my bed. It seemed to be growing in size. At the same time it was giving off a strong light of its own in spite of the fact that the moonlight shining through the window was very bright.

As I watched the glowing mist, it seemed to be growing in size and density until it reached four or five feet across. There was one peculiar characteristic and that the mist seemed to be confined inside a barrier. Let me explain, it was swirling around all the time and becoming denser but at the same time it was confined, as it were inside a glass globe. After a while I plucked up courage and jumped out of bed and ran over to the door to switch on the overhead light.

I sat on the side of the bed wondering what to do next. I was feeling very frightened to say the least. I eventually decided to put out the light and get back in bed, as the room was extremely cold, there being no central heating in the house.
I lay in bed thinking that it must have been my imagination when the same thing happened again. The same swirling, mist giving out the same phosphorescent glow and still confined inside that invisible globe. This time it increased in size much more slowly than before. All the time I was watching it, absolutely terrified, but I felt compelled to keep it under observation.

After a while I put my head under the bed clothes as it had still not gone away. Eventually I must have fallen asleep because the next thing that I knew was that it was morning and time to get up for breakfast.
I do not know what it was that I saw that night, but there are two things that I am certain of and they are that it was not my imagination, and that it was evil because there was a very

loathsome feeling about it.

Sometime afterwards, meaning several years later, I did find out that the wife of the owner, namely our hostess, unknown to her husband and family or us, had dealings with the occult. Could this be something to do with it?

In 1986, a daughter of the owner asked me to accompany her to 'Bleak House', to collect some belongings of her mother who had just died. She told me that she was afraid to go to the house on her own, having spent every day for the last two weeks packing up her mother's belongings. "There is something very evil in that house", she told me. "I cannot spend another minute there on my own". She said that she always made a point on leaving the house before darkness fell.

Anyway, I went with her to the house and as soon as I entered the main entrance hall I felt very uncomfortable. She asked me to go upstairs to collect some items for her, which I did. As soon as I set foot on the first floor landing I had a feeling of extreme dread. My feet felt as if they were too heavy for my legs.

The further I walked away from the staircase onto the first floor the worse I felt. I have heard of people having a hair raising experience, well up to that day I thought that it was a metaphorical figure of speech. I can honestly say that I felt a tingling sensation running over my scalp.

As soon as I had collected the items, I left the first floor via the stairs and felt much more comfortable, although I did not feel entirely at ease until I had left the house.

There is no doubt in my mind that there is or was at the time a presence in that house. It was a presence of the most unpleasant kind and I am sure that it was not of this world.
The old rectory was typical of a large Victorian house with numerous large rooms, each with high ceilings; very cold and draughty in the winter. When in that house, I felt that I was too far from the living and much too close to the dead.

Whilst doing my army basic training at the R.E.M.E. Training Depot which was at 'Poperinghe Barracks' in the Berkshire village of Arborfield, I also had a very strange experience.

One night I got out of bed to go to the toilet and looked at my watch and it showed 11.30 pm. I returned to my bed which was just inside the door of the barrack room, on the left by the light switches. I had not yet been asleep and was perfectly sober.

I suppose that I had been in the barrack room for about ten minutes or so when the door opened. I saw a figure enter the room and walk up the central aisle, between the two rows of beds. I could see it clearly in the bright moonlight that was shining through the windows. The figure went up to one of the steel lockers, opened it and started rummaging around inside it. Thinking that it was someone trying to steal from one of my colleagues, I jumped out of bed and switched on the electric light. There was no one there at all. The figure had completely disappeared.

The following morning, I found out that three other people in the barrack room had also seen the person walk into barrack room. They saw them rummage inside the locker, their reports tallied more or less with what I had witnessed. So I could not have imagined the incident. This strange occurrence happened in 1962.

There is another strange experience from my army days that I would like to mention. I was posted on the permanent staff of the R.E.M.E. School of Electronic Engineering at Hazebrouck Barracks also in Arborfield.

On the night in question I was on guard duty and had to patrol, with a colleague, the neighbouring 'Beaulieu Barracks', which was located about half a mile away. It was a mostly disused barracks with a lot of empty huts known as 'spiders'. As we approached the centre of the camp we both saw a person walking towards us and then walk between two legs of one particular hut. We both shone our torches onto the figure as we thought that it was an intruder. The moonlight was very bright that night and the security lights were on throughout the camp, so there was no mistaking anything else for a person.

Both my companion and I ran towards the spot where the figure went and when we arrived there was no one there at all. There was no way that the figure could escape without us noticing it. There was no door into the building and all the windows were fastened securely.

There had been, over the years, many strange happenings in that place; it seemed to have a rather unsavoury reputation. About two hours later we were walking along the edge of the parade ground when we both heard what sounded like someone marching across the parade ground in hobnailed army boots. Despite the fact that the whole area was illuminated by the perimeter lights, we could not see anyone at all. The invisible marcher seemed to pass within about twenty feet or so of where we were standing, pass and gradually fade away.

In more recent years I have experienced a couple of minor but interesting incidents for which I can find no rational explanation. I live in a cottage in the heart of The Dorset countryside. One evening, as I was going to bed, I heard a noise coming from inside the bedroom fireplace. The grate had a piece of plywood over the front of it to stop draughts coming down the chimney. I did not use the fireplace at all. The noise, sounded as if two or three birds had fallen down the chimney and were fighting or flapping about and were unable to escape. The noise was certainly very loud and coming from the fireplace.

I immediately removed the piece of plywood that was covering the opening and expected to see a bird or two fly out. There was nothing there at all, not even one bird. I replaced the wood and almost immediately the same thing happened again, the flapping and scratching sound; just as loud. Again, I removed the plywood cover and again there was nothing visible to account for the noise. On both occasions, the noise stopped immediately when the cover was removed.

In 1985, I was visiting the owner of a very large and isolated country house in North Dorset. The building was being restored at the time and the owner, whom I know well, wished to show me the near completed restoration work. There was no furniture in the house at the time and the only contents were the workmen's tools and equipment. It was on a Saturday morning so the workmen were not there. Just as I was about to say goodbye to the owner and his wife and leave there was a tremendous crashing sound which sounded as if thousands of glass bottles had been dropped onto a stone floor from a great height. It was really deafening.

We immediately searched the whole building from attic to cellar. But were unable to find anything to account for the noise. Everything was as it should have been, all in order.

I have had an interest in mysteries and the unexplained for many years. I think that most people, if they are to be honest with themselves, are intrigued with mysteries. The supernatural is a veil through which we cannot see, it is a door for which we have no key.

Kate's story

I would like to tell you about my experience at the ghost hunt in the black cat bar, on the back stairs that lead up to the road at the front of the pub. I was asked to come to see what I made of the activities that were being sensed on the back stairs. The first thing that happened when I got to the stairs was my right ear started to hurt me. I sensed a girl aged about 6 or 7, with very dark hair and dark brown eyes. She was holding a toy wooden sailing ship. I asked her about it and she said that her father had given it to her because he used to be away a lot on the sea. She said that she liked her dad but that she wanted her mum.

She looked unusually small for her age and I felt her hold onto the crux of my right arm. I asked her why she was there and I got the sense that she was looking for her mother. I asked her why she hadn't passed over to the other side to see her mum and she said that she doesn't know who her mum is. I felt that her mother had died when this girl was very young. I asked her whether she wanted to meet her mum and go to her on the other side. She agreed and at this point, one of the women present felt her legs shake and she went tearful. She said that she had sensed this girl's older sister there earlier before I arrived and then I remarked that this little girl wanted to sit on this woman's lap as she felt she was like an elder sister.

During these exchanges, 4 of us felt very cold shivers run through us at exactly the same time. I asked my spirit guide to find this girl's mother and I saw a narrow shaft of light in my mind's eye at the top of the stairs to the left. There stood a woman in a candy striped long skirt and blouse and bolero jacket. She looked very pretty like this girl, with dark hair and dark eyes. She looked smart and I am guessing now that the era would have been 1820, possibly earlier. She had a straw boater hat and looked like she was in her early 20's.

Before I could even give instructions for this girl to go to her mother, she had run up the stairs to her. The women with the crystals found that the crystals had stopped moving and I could feel that she had gone. It was very intense and an emotional experience for us all.

Someone asked whether there was anyone else still there. I assumed that the older sister would have also gone to her mother at this moment, but she was still present.

My next experience was in the other ladies' loo which is at the bottom of the kitchen steps. As I stood in the middle cubicle, again I felt a hand push down on my head slightly to the right hand side of the top of my head. I got the impression this was a male energy and was just being mischievous. I also felt myself being pulled backwards but there was no nastiness here - just mischief!

I had the urge to sit on the table under the lights on the pillar in the bottom bar. Darren was sat there originally and nothing had happened. He told me that people had been pushed off there before and I wanted to find out more. The moment I sat down on the table and faced the bar-side wall, I felt a cold sharp jab in my lower back. It pushed me forward but I stayed on the table. I asked, "Who did that?" and I immediately got jabbed again but more on the left hand side of my lower back. I said to stop that and asked not to be pushed off the table either. As soon as I asked that, he (by then I had sensed that this was the spirit of a frustrated man, aged about 32) electrocuted my left arm which made me yelp in pain and jump off the table! I sat back down and asked, "Who did this?" and he did it again. I asked him to stop it because actually, I am a nice person and I don't deserve that treatment. I said that I may be able to help him if he wanted help.

All the time I was sat there I got the real powerful feeling that this man was stood behind me and kept swinging around to see if he was! I asked him about himself and he put a picture of an iron in my mind's eye and he said he is very strong. When he said this, it felt as if my left eye was crying and I felt sad. I saw a picture of him and he was wearing a cream coloured jumper in the 60's style, a slight crew neck. He had gingery blonde hair which was thick and a bit wavy.

I asked him if there was anyone he would like to meet from the other side and he immediately said his wife, Mandy. I asked if he would like to pass over to be with her. He said yes and I asked my spirit guide to find Mandy to come and fetch him. It happened very quickly. I saw a shaft of light and Mandy (dark brown hair, very pretty, petite lady) came through with her mother. Her mother was 'enabling' her to come through.

This could be why he found it difficult to pass over before

because he was adamant that he didn't want to be picked up by anyone else but Mandy but she was not able to do this at the time. As soon as she was there, I felt him take over my left arm and then take over my left leg and foot. This was very peculiar because it really did not feel like my own and it was moving itself. This has happened before to me when spirits come close but not to this extent. He was a very strong physical presence. I felt my right eye fill with tears, which is a reaction to the light of Mandy and her mum and the emotion from her. I then felt my left side of my face go fuzzy and it felt like not mine. This is when someone said that she could see half the face of a man with chiselled jaw take over that side of my face.

I said "Ok, you are showing me that you are here", and I gave him instructions about how to pass over. I held Mandy's hand from the other side and I asked him (guessing his name was Jim at this point, but not definite) to hold onto my hand and I was going to join their hands together to connect them up. This is when he moved my hand himself and he slowly moved his hand (ha - it was mine but didn't feel like it!) towards my right hand. I encouraged him all the way until he made my body twist off the table and walk towards where Mandy was.

He stretched his hand outwards and they held hands and stayed like that for about 10 seconds and then I felt the connection go and I had my body back. My left side was tingly and slightly painful. It was then when he had passed over, that I got the sense that his wife had died when she was young and that he never got over it. He wanted to be picked up by her when he died but could not because there was no-one to enable her to do this. He had no sense of time and didn't realize that he had been jabbing people for so long. He wanted to world to know that he was strong but underneath he was very sad. He saw this as a weakness and enjoyed poking people to prove his strength. He was not a bully but he was determined to cover up his sadness with strength.

The Dick Wittington pub

One night me and my friend Norman Ferguson, who was the manager there, did an overnight investigation. This particular night was very active and eerie as I recall, and we were all a bit spooked out.

We split up and went our different ways. Norman walked downstairs from the bar towards the door to the black cat bar, which was shut but had a glass front. Jamie, who was one of the young bar staff, was in front of Norman when, just as he was about to open the door, a face appeared, staring at him.

Well, you can imagine Jamie screamed like a banshee, which in turn scared Norman behind him and the pair of them started to run back up to the bar, only to find out later it was one of my team members just about to open the door herself, saw Jamie and screamed and ran the other way!

All this was perfect timing but not intentional as we did not do this on our investigations, but it was so funny. When everyone had calmed down, we started laughing about it and very often remember that night and burst out laughing again.

Gloucester Docks
The cursed ship

Some ships just seem to be cursed with bad luck. in

Gloucester docks in 1861, a captain took charge of his first sailing vessel. 48 hours after he took command, he died suddenly.

The vessel left Gloucester docks and struck a fishing weir leaving a gash in its hull. It returned to Gloucester for repairs where the vessel suffered a fire which broke out on board. After being repaired yet again, it set sail only to collide with another ship. Finally, in 1867 the vessel was again restored and was sold to an American company who sailed it to the south of America and sold it to an American captain in 1872. It disappeared at sea and was never seen again.

Once upon a time (are you sitting comfortably?), a ship crew member noticed a rather dilapidated vessel anchored in Gloucester Docks. It looked like it was ready for the knacker's yard.

One night he noticed a faint light coming from one of the port holes, so he decided to walk over and have a look. As he climbed aboard the deserted ship he felt uneasy. He opened the door to the crew's cabin and was confronted by a man. He wore a mustard coloured coat and a cap pulled over his eyes, BUT he was floating 3 feet above the ground. The terrified sailor ran back to his own ship immediately.

The next night he was worried by what he had seen. He had to go back and check it out. He opened the door and no one was there. Had someone previously hung themselves? Was he seeing things? He didn't know what to think.

 he sailor told his shipmates all about the two nights, and they laughed at him and said to him "What ship?" He pointed out to them in the direction he had saw the ship and as he turned there was no ship. And according to his shipmates, there never was. "Ye been on the rum too much me hearty" his shipmates roared. Around 1885, a wooden barque (pronounced bark) from Spain docked in the Reynolds quay near what is known as the 'G' warehouse (the back of the Mariners Church). The cargo contained, amongst other things, a load of long poles of onions which would last a good housewife long enough until the next visit of the Spanish sailors.

The Spanish sailors were well known for their Mediterranean temperament. They also had a reputation for drinking, fighting, and womanising with their dark eyes and charm. One night, the reason is not known, two Spaniards fell into a disagreement with other sailors from another visiting vessel. A violent fight broke out, drink was a main cause of the severity of the quarrel (no change today then). Dawn broke out and the grisly sight was seen on the deck of the Spanish ship. Strung up from the yardarm, and swinging by their feet were the bodies of two men. Their throats had been cut. The drained corpses swayed lifeless in the morning chill. Their blood spilled on the deck. Their unfortunate mates had the unpleasant task of cutting them down. Sometimes, on a misty evening in the quay, the whole area becomes very still. A ghostly wooden barque comes into view and for a fleeting moment the bodies of the two sailors can be seen again hanging from the yardarm.

James Broslin's story

I always feel there's a presence at my home number 25 Ashgrove Avenue. I always have this feeling that I am being watched, and when I am in the kitchen washing up or doing any cooking, I feel sometimes that there is someone stood behind me looking over my shoulder. The temperature in some parts in house, in particular the living room, drops really icy cold. I have never seen any apparitions. However, I feel there is something there. Nothing malevolent mind.

The Maples, Abbeymead, Gloucester
Sarah Barr, June 2010

My husband and I moved into our house in August 2004. About a year after we moved in, strange things started to happen such as the DVD player switching itself on at 4 am most mornings. Because it has integrated Freeview and separate speakers from the telly, I would frequently wake up to someone talking downstairs. It was usually one of the news channels.

Whilst sitting on the sofa, I have seen a dark shape out of the corner of my eye coming down the stairs. The dog frequently stares with her ears pricked forward at a particular spot in the lounge. She also watches the stairs and has been known to put her hackles up and growl when there appears to be nothing there.

My sister has been house sitting while we've been away and has been woken in the middle of the night by someone shouting in her ear.

The most significant thing that happened to me was one day when I took the dog to the vets. My husband was due to come with me but was late home from work, so I took her on my own. When I returned home, I pulled up on the drive and saw someone standing in the kitchen. My immediate thought was that my husband was home, but when I went to open the front door it was still locked. I went in and there was no one there. He arrived home about 10 minutes later. Before I had gone out, I had put the washing machine on. When I got home, it was switched off halfway through the cycle. I thought maybe the door had knocked it, but when I moved the door against the machine, the button was nowhere near it.

I don't get any bad feeling with the house, in fact my sister and I affectionately refer to "him" as Caspar, because we feel he's a friendly ghost. Out of curiosity, I have thought about asking a medium to come in and see who it is, but equally as I don't feel threatened, I don't want to risk upsetting him. My husband doesn't believe there is anything there. However, if I go out and come home late and he has gone to bed, I will always find a trail of lights left on!

Rob Flory's story

Running parallel to Southgate Street is a road named Ladybellegate Street. Around 25 years ago, my dad stayed after a night out in a friend's flat who lived down there. The flats where converted from houses at some point. In the early hours of the morning, he woke to use the bathroom and had to leave that level of the block and descend to a lower level where the toilets were located. As he walked down the stairs, through a window he could see the Blackfriars and thought to himself how creepy it looked at that time of night when there was no one else around. The following day, he mentioned his late night expedition to the toilets to his friend that he was staying with. His response to my dad's comment was that there were far more eerie goings on in the flat itself. He went on to explain how his young daughter was woken regularly in tears and often spoke of a "man" who she would see in there and who would sit in a chair. They dismissed this as just her imagination but were still concerned as it was clearly upsetting her. Finally, one day they were looking through books or papers and saw pictures of monks, to which their daughter pointed and said to them "there's the man, the man that comes" (or words to that effect). After hearing this and seeing their daughter lose sleep over it, they decided to have the house "cleaned". A priest came and when he finished what he came to do he told them that he could not move what was in the flat but assured them that it meant no harm. With their daughter waking in the night crying and losing sleep they were eventually relocated to new accommodation.

Cafe Rene 2009

On one of my ghost walks one night, I took 18 people down into 'deep six ' a very spooky area past the cellar bar which is located underneath the main bar and even beyond that. While I was talking to my group and shining my torch around, suddenly to everyone's shock, we all saw from the beam of my torch, a small stone thrown from directly behind me and hit a lady on her arm. Her daughter said another one was also thrown but we only saw the first one. The strange thing was, firstly this has NEVER happened before on any of my walks or in deep six, and secondly it came from and area where I was stood that had a three to four feet drop directly behind me. Yet we all saw the trajectory of the stone which was straight across my shoulder, as if someone was stood directly behind me.

I of course asked who was there and shone my torch all around, but no one answered me. I can tell you in all honesty that did freak me out for quite some time afterwards. I think it is the not knowing that frightens us. Yes, yes. I know. Why do I do it then I hear you ask. Well simply because I enjoy it and I would like to know more. However, having experienced that happening and thinking a few weeks later, ok I'm over that now, I was shocked again when I was taking another group of people into deep six. As soon as I opened the door and turned the light on, myself and three other people heard this very sudden crash and we all saw a dark shadow, the size of a small dog (no, not a cat or rat) jump as if coming from the ceiling onto a table and scurrying away towards the same area the stone was thrown weeks earlier. This is at the very bottom of this very large area and we were only just at the doorway coming into the room. I cannot explain it at all. At first, I thought it was a dog or some animal that had got in and got trapped down there, but there is no other way into deep six, other than the way we come in.

This disturbed me even more than the stone being thrown. All the time I was talking to my group I was shining my torch around trying to see what on earth it was that we saw, but, nothing more happened. Since then, people have been down there, but as yet, nothing further has happened. Yet!

We have also heard three very faint whistles back, in response to our three whistles. Everyone was accounted for to prove it was not any of us.

We have had people with brand new batteries just put in their torches and cameras etc. yet completely drain in that area. But as soon as we go out of that room and back upstairs, the batteries are working and are fully charged.

I bet some of you are wondering 'what's Lyn on about, deep

six'? Well the owner, Paul Soden and all the staff, have named it so because it is approximately six feet underground right under the forecourt and outside seating areas. It can be a very creepy place at times, as some of you will know if you have been down there.

My Story of St. Briavels Castle

I have stayed at the Castle a couple of times now and it is a very active place. I stayed in the Oubliette room, which means 'to forget' in French. It is where prisoners were thrown down in to a deep well, like pit, and left to die. It has an iron grid over it now for safety reasons. This room has been known to have a spirit that tugs at the bed clothes, which I wasn't told about until the next day.

In the night, I was very restless and couldn't sleep as I felt someone was in the room. I eventually dozed off, only to experience that someone was tugging at my bed clothes over my feet and woke me up.

I couldn't wait until it got light and went to find anyone else that was awake. I was surprised to find a few were. I told everyone what had happened and most of them laughed and said that always happens in that room and in the bed I was in. "Thanks people" I said.

Craig Y Nos In Wales

This small estate in the mountains of Wales appealed to Madam Adelina Juana Maria Patti, who bought the castle and surrounding park land for £3500. The prima Donna had reached the soaring heights of a spectacular career and was to spend the rest of her life at Craig-y-nos, leaving to sing in the premier opera house of Europe and elsewhere, captivating the world with her flawless soprano voice.

I have visited this wonderful Castle on a couple of occasions with some friends for a 'paranormal ' nigh. We were not disappointed on both occasions. I still remember our visit very well.

We toured around the inside of the Castle in various different places and learnt the history of the castle, once being a TB hospital many years ago, and several other occupants in its time including the famous opera singer Adelina Patti.

We went into the Theatre where Adelina sang and did a quiet vigil for a while. Then we called out, asking if there was anyone there. Quite a few of us saw sparkly lights, which we call 'spirit' lights, around the stage and down the steps from the stage leading down into where the audiences would have sat.

We decided to try and sing one of her favourite songs 'There's no place like home'. To our surprise, we found that when we got to the high notes, we could actually sing them even though none of us were singers.

Suddenly our walkie talkies went off and it was another group that had gone upstairs to another part of the building. They were asking us if we could hear loud singing. We laughed and said "Yes, that was us". They replied, "It didn't sound like any of you, as it sounded good." (blooming cheek) haha.

We then went upstairs and the other team came down. We

were in a part of the old TB hospital doing an experiment of table tipping, where 4 of us had placed our hands on top of the table visible for everyone else to see that we were not moving table ourselves.

The medium with us was asking questions out loud for any spirits to come forward and talk to us by moving the table. The table started to move eventually, swaying from side to side then round and round.

I was watching outside the circle of people that were doing this experiment and then the medium was called away to another room. Someone needed his help. Not a spirit, a person had felt ill. So off he went, but before he went he said "Carry on. Ask questions but one at a time. Don't bombard the spirit with too many people talking all at once."

He had not been gone long and the table was still tilting when several people started asking the spirit questions and not really waiting for the answers before asking another question. I found myself getting very frustrated and agitated, then angry. I could not explain it and was trying to control myself.

All of a sudden, I shouted at everyone to stop, the spirit had had enough and was getting angry. I had never met some of these people before, yet here I was, shouting at them.
Just then, the Medium came back and said that I was right, the spirit had had enough of all the questions and used my voice to tell them to stop. And we stopped and moved on to another room.

Another time, my friend Caroline and I stayed for two nights in the old part of the castle. We shared a room where we each had a single bed for the night.

In the night, Caroline had woken up as she felt that someone was in the room with us. She looked over at me and saw, what she described as a nurse trying to tuck me into bed, but I was fast asleep and was unaware of this. She said in my sleep I was tugging at my bed clothes, trying to pull them up and also saying, in a not very nice way (yes you can guess), "Leave me alone". Then the nurse disappeared. In the morning, Caroline told me what had happened and was laughing at the language I was using. I had no idea what had happened or what I had said until she told me. Very strange.

The next night we were staying in the bunk beds in the dormitory over on the other side of the castle in the newer part. This is where Caroline and I were meeting our other friends Nicky, Lisa, Nessa and Trevina and joining more people for another investigation that night. Again, an eventual evening with sounds and shadows we couldn't explain. We then all went to bed, all of us in the same room.

I couldn't believe it when Nicky and Nellie told me they saw me pulling the clothes back over me yet again and cursing whoever was tugging at my sheets. Two nights in a row, what on earth was going on and why me, why not any of the others?

For a long time, I couldn't figure out what that was all about and then, just like that, it came to me. Maybe the nurse was tucking me in as my mother had TB In her early 20's and after all, it was once a Tb hospital. Who knows. Will I ever know! Certainly a weekend I will never forget.

Rhonda Lytle Sheppard's story
New Inn: Cellar with Dave Mason

Dave and I decided to do a vigil in the cellar as there had been a lot of activity reported there. Things started off quiet, but then we received "knocks" to answers of our questions (once for yes, twice for no). We began to see lights, like sparks, and they seemed to centre in one area and take shape. During this time, we also saw white flashes. It's important to add there are no windows, the door was closed and all lights were off. Suddenly, we saw the shape of a shoulder and an arm. This then disappeared and we then saw a torso. We realized someone was trying very hard to appear and we asked them to use our energy. We soon saw the face of a boy who turned to smile at me, then turned to David and gave him a huge grin! David, who is quite strong of build, attempted to lean to the side to get his camera but was forcefully yanked away from it!

The boy we "met" in the cellar was named Thomas. He said his parents worked upstairs, which would mean they were possibly management at one time. A look at records showed there was a man named Thomas and his wife running the New Inn at one point and they had a son. Thomas wasn't able to appear in full form, though he did try. What he was able to show looked as if a person was standing there. But as he got weaker from trying to fully appear, he became more opaque.

About a week later, I took a trigger object into the cellar, a yellow toy car. I placed it behind a set of large boilers where nobody goes and circled it with a wire I found. I went back a few times and at first the toy car remained. Then one day I went down to find the toy car gone. I hadn't told anybody about placing the trigger object there, and when asked, nobody had gone behind the boilers (staff found the cellar frightening) and were unaware of the item I placed there.

Room 109: After an event at the New Inn, I opted to stay overnight and booked a room. I had settled in comfortably and was watching TV when suddenly the screen went a fuzzy grey and I could see shapes moving on the screen. My initial thought was it was a problem with the tube or something along those lines. I decided I'd turn off the TV and let the staff know in the morning. As I went to turn off the TV, I decided I should also unplug it and that's when I saw the plug. It was pulled almost all the way out, leaning backward and just hovering there. I hadn't pulled the plug as I had been watching TV from bed. The plug was also pulled so far out of the socket that the TV should have just gone blank instead of the fuzzy grey with moving shapes! I pushed the plug back in and the TV went back to working normally. When I told the staff about it, I was told it had occurred before.

Gloucester's Paranormal Investigation Services (GPIS)
St. Catherine's, Matson, July 2016

Ed and Paul have always had an interest in the paranormal. One night in July, they decided to venture up to St. Catherine's graveyard with only an EVP (Electronic voice phenomenon) recorder and a camera. What they captured that night on EVP of a man's voice saying, "So help me god", and pictures of what could be described as and documented as 'Grey lady', has to be the inspiration behind them setting up GPIS.

Since then they have investigated various other locations such as The Gloucester Antiques Centre, Age Concern UK,

The Dick Wittingham and The Fleece, with some of these historical places and buildings having never been investigated before.

Gloucester Antiques Centre, 26 Westgate street

Ed and Paul had the opportunity to be able to investigate this historical building set in Westgate Street over a period of three months. Some of their evidence has been covered by The Citizen newspaper and Gloucestershire Live.

Although not obvious from the street with its Georgian frontage, this building is said to be the finest example in Britain of a timber framed town house, and as such is a Grade I listed building. Dating back to 1560, it was once the hall of the Grocer's Guild, the mansion house of a Mayor of Gloucester and, in the 19th century a lodging for assize judges. It was alledged to have been the headquarters of Colonel Edward Massie during the siege of Gloucester in 1643, when he held the city against the King.

A voice of an Irishman called Michael, the voice of a woman called Mary and Carol, the name of a child saying 'daddy' have all been captured by Ed and Paul on spirit box and camera audio, amongst other evidence, to suggest that 26 Westgate Street is haunted. They have also captured orbs and strange light anomalies travelling up the stairs into the ceiling.

Ed and Paul would like to thank Cathy Williams, Director of the Gloucester Antiques Centre for giving them the opportunity to investigate such an interesting piece of history, and also for what they have managed to document.

"It has been an amazing experience and so interesting to learn about the history associated with this building. Also, we would like to say thank you to Lyn Cinderey for her guidance and for kindly giving us the opportunity to contribute to her book.
Peace and happiness, love and light
GPIS".

In conclusion, I hope you all enjoy my book and I have given you some food for thought. If we don't write these things down, it will be a great shame and the people in the future will not know about us, the things that happened to us, what we did or what we think.

So many times, I have read 'History' books and sometimes very little small details left out have made me curious. That is why I have tried to give you more information and also inspired you into another way of thinking of life after death.
Of course, this is only my opinion. Each to your own beliefs.

Since writing this book, I have met a really lovely lady named Angela Gillett, who has inspired me greatly and helped me further into my beliefs. Angela has taught me many wonderful things and I thank her so much. Angela works with the Angels on the Angelic Realm and now so do I. My Life has changed so much for the better and I feel whole and complete. It's amazing.

I feel over the years I have lived my life in many different stages.

I love helping people by giving them Crystal Readings, another tool of communicating with spirit, and the information coming through is truly wonderful for me, but more importantly for the person I'm reading for.

I have sensed, seen, heard and communicated with Spirit now for many years. I see things in my Crystals that I must say, amuses me and astounds me sometimes. But as the reading is not for me, I have to give it to the person I'm reading for and find that they resonate with what I see.

I feel I am at peace within myself now and know that my sister Mo. brother Pete, Mum, Dad, Gran and friend Leanne and A.M. and all my relations in the 'BIG' house, as I call it, are guiding me and the Angels of course, to hopefully be a better person. A stronger person so that I can give mine and their love to whoever needs it.

Thank you all

Love Lyn xx